POEMS WORTH SAVING
by
Baxter Black

**Illustrated by
Bob Black
Don Gill
Dave Holl
Charlie Marsh
Etienne "A-10" Etcheverry
&
Bill Patterson**

Copyright ©2013 by Baxter Black

Published by: Coyote Cowboy Company
PO Box 2190
Benson, AZ 85602
baxterblack.com

Cover and book design by Becky Harvey

LIBRARY OF CONGRESS CATALOGING IN PUBLICATION DATA:
Main entry under:
Cowboy Poetry

Bibliography: p
1. Poems Worth Saving
2. Poetry-Cowboy
3. Cowboy-Poetry
4. Humor-Cowboy

I. Black, Baxter, 1945-
Library of Congress #2013942731
ISBN-13: 978-0939343-57-7

OTHER BOOKS BY BAXTER
The Cowboy and His Dog
A Rider, A Roper, And A Heck'uva Windmill Man
On The Edge Of Common Sense, The Best So Far
Doc, While Yer Here
Buckaroo History
Coyote Cowboy Poetry
Croutons On A Cow Pie
The Buckskin Mare
Cowboy Standard Time
Croutons On A Cow Pie, Vol 2
Hey, Cowboy, Wanna Get Lucky? (Crown Publishing, Inc.)
Dunny And The Duck
Cow Attack
Cactus Tracks And Cowboy Philosophy (Crown Publishing, Inc.)
A Cowful Of Cowboy Poetry
Horseshoes, Cowsocks And Duckfeet (Crown Publishing, Inc.)
Ag Man The Comic Book
Hey, Cowgirl, Need A Ride? (Crown Publishing, Inc.)
Blazin' Bloats & Cows On Fire!
The World According To Baxter Black: Quips, Quirks & Quotes
The Back Page (Western Horseman Books)
Lessons From A Desperado Poet (TwoDot)
Herbert's Night Off
Reindeer Flu
Ride, Cowboy, Ride! Eight Seconds Ain't That Long (TwoDot)

"Rhythm and rhyme are accessible to anyone who possesses the blessing of language, but most of us occupy a world that is out of rhythm and doesn't rhyme.

With Baxter, " . . . we are suddenly confronted by a re-arrangement of the language we speak everyday. We recognize the words, but he gives them an order we never dreamed was there."
- **John Erickson, writer and rancher**

" . . . Baxter Black meanders along an incongruous stream of creative unconsciousness, surveying side channels of irrationality. To paraphrase Otto von Bismark, BB dog paddles on the stormy waves of phrase. Nothing stems his tide." - **Dr. Bob Howdy, newspaper man**

"He is the only famous person I know who's just one of us."
- **Bill Pfeil, Alabama farmer**

"He can turn a birthday cake into a four-alarm fire!"
- **Mrs. Rath, his 8th grade teacher**

Disclaimer by author:
It is quite embarrassing to receive reviews that are so eloquent they overshadow the talents they praise. It rings of King David praising President Buchanan's acceptance speech in his Psalms. You notice there is no mention of Buchanan in the Old Testament.

INTRODUCTION

It would be fair to say that I didn't find cowboy poetry, it found me. I was a busy, contented, hard workin' large animal veterinarian when cowboy poetry hijacked my career. I had made an amateurish attempt at writing songs as a young man and I have always been good tellin' stories. As I traveled the countryside treating animals, I would hear stories and jokes, baxterize them and tell them at the next ranch or feedlot I went to! Then one day I decided to put a story to rhyme and it worked . . . meaning, the cowboys loved it!

I had no models, to speak of. I was not really aware of the Gail Gardner's or Badger Clark's and I paid very little attention to the Victorian poets in English Class. So my poetry was more like poor song writing. Then, by chance, I was introduced to the poetry of Carlos Ashley from Texas and Banjo Paterson from Australia. It was epiphenal!

I saw what it was supposed to look like, and how it should sound.

Granted, I still cannot write with their brilliance and clarity, but I'm funny, and I can write funny poetry, and that is enough for me.

I make a living doing agricultural banquets. When I began, rural ag speakers like Jerry Clower, Ace Reid, Doc Blakely and Earl Butts were the pro's. I was pleased to be called as their second or third choice, ie. "We tried to get Ace but he was busy...you don't charge much, do ya?"

I related more to Ace than the others. He was a Texas cartoonist who picked on cowboys, ranchers, farmers, bankers, ropers, rodeo hands, feed salesmen, horse traders, veterinarians, cattle buyers, cow dogs and drought. I'd say that pretty much describes my audience, as well. I'm just carrying on the tradition.

This book is a collection. As President Franklin D. Roosevelt said when asked how many books he had written in his lifetime, he mulled briefly then replied, "Altogether . . . too many."

In my case, I can't keep them all in print. It's expensive, and I think it is illegal in some states.

So, suffice it to say this is the first sort. I have chosen the title "Poems Worth Saving" obviously, to leave room for a sequel, "Poems Not Worth Saving."

I have been blessed by the good Lord to live in the company of folks I admire and care about. People of the land, I give you my hand, you're the salt of the Earth, Amen.

TABLE OF CONTENTS:

CHAPTER 1
COWBOY
MENTALITY

Romantical crooners sing western songs about the life of the cowboy, his love of his horse, and his ability to rescue the rancher's daughter. They hold him to an idolic standard.

His statue stands for honesty and bravery, a man to reckon with. They ignore his qualities of stubbornness, belligerence, superstition, and a need to do something the hard way, even if he has to climb over the easy way, to do it!

They face decisions like: "Should I let my broken arm heal or should I repel down the face of Mt. Everest on a dare?"

Psychologists, no doubt, have troublesome sounding names for people who color outside the lines, will cut off their nose to spite their face, and prefer a game with no out-of-bounds.

I have been a part of the world of cowboys long enough to be one, I guess. I look back on the memories of the times I chose the hard way to go, without even looking at the menu. A quick replay of some of the close calls that I regularly have had in my life makes me want to fast-forward the movie so I won't have to think about how stupid I was!

The best way a lay psychotherapist could get a sense of the cowboy mentality would be to analyze and understand this joke; Hold your hand up in front of your face and challenge your friend, "Bet you can't hit my hand before I move it!"

Unfortunately, I am still under the influence of the cowboy way of thinking. This chapter is littered with examples of when our hero takes the path that says "Road Closed!"

THE SPUR

I came to a low water crossing
Where the trails converged near the bank
All by itself I spotted a spur
That lay buried plum up to the shank.

I kicked at the dirt all around it
But its mate was not to be found
Then I wondered just what circumstances
Had led to the spur in the ground.

This trail, no doubt, had been traveled
By sinner and saint in the past
And the spur was a quiet reminder
That leather and muscle don't last.

It might have belonged to a bandit
Who was hanged by the neck from a tree,
A settler who drowned on his way to the west;
A drifter who longed to breathe free.

It might have belonged to a cowpoke
Who bucked off a renegade bronc
Or lost by two lovers one romantic night
On the way back from some honky tonk.

A trapper, a scout, a brave buckaroo,
A panner who died for his claim,
The spur stood alone, an unexplained story,
A headstone awaiting a name.

I finally unraveled the mystery.
My answer was there in the sands
The tracks of his horse went round in a circle.
The spur was a one leg-ged man's!

Illustration: Bob Black

VANISHING BREED?

They call'em a vanishing breed.
They write books and take pictures
and talk like they're all dyin' out.
Like dinosaurs goin' to seed
But that's my friends yer talkin' about.

Like Tex from Juniper Mountain.
He carved out a way of life
where only the toughest prevail.
He's sixty-seven an' countin'
His sons now follow his trail.

And Mike who still ain't got married.
At home in the seat of a saddle,
a sagebrush aristocrat.
I reckon that's how he'll be buried;
A'horseback, still wearin' his hat.

There's Bryan, Albert and Floyd.
Cowmen as good as the legends
to whom their livelihood's linked.
Who'd be just a little annoyed
To know they're considered extinct.

Some say they're endangered species
Destined to fade into footnotes
like ropes that never get throwed.
To that I reply, "Bull Feces!"
They're just hard to see from the road.

ॐ

TALK ABOUT TOUGH!

I've listened to you varmints braggin'
'Bout cowboys, the toughest you've known,
But the first liar don't have a chance, boys,
'Cause I knew one tough to the bone.

He came out from someplace in Kansas
In truth he was hard to dislike,

'Cause he weren't really mean, just hard headed.
They called him Peewilliker Mike.

When the weather got down below freezin'
Why, he'd never cover his ears.
So now each one looks like a knothole
'Cause pieces broke off through the years.

A she-bear invaded his camp once,
Insisted on sharin' his plate.
He saved the last of his biscuit
Though now he can jes' count to eight.

He used to have both of his elbows,
A forehead without so much slope,
'Til a cow jerked him outta the saddle. . .
He wouldn't let go of the rope.

He's faster than most fixin' fences
Though it's almost beyond belief,
'Cause he keeps both hands free fer poundin'
By stretchin' the wire with his teeth.

And what's more he don't use a hammer!
Drives nails with the back of his hand.
But this last thing I'm fixin' to tell ya
Will prove that there's no tougher man.

While pushin' a cow to the home ranch
Adrift in a cowboy's dreams,
A rattlesnake up and surprised him,
His horse came apart at the seams!

He bucked clean outta the saddle
So high that his bad breath condensed,
An' come down a cussin' and lighted
Astraddle a dang bob wire fence.

It cut'im right up to the buckle
Between his feet and his chin,
He jes' let his stirrups out longer
And rode his ol' pony on in.

ANONYMOUS END

I'm here at an old pal's funeral
Not too many people have come
Just a few of us boys from the outfit
So he don't go out like a bum.

Seems like I've known him forever
As I look back over the years
We've rode several wagons together
And shared a couple of beers.

He never quite made it to foreman
But then, of course, neither have I.
He always sorta stayed to the center
Just kind of a regular guy.

He'd always chip in for a party
Though he was never one to get loud.
Everything that he did was just average
He never stood out in a crowd.

He was fair with a rope and a rifle,
He was never early or late.
In the pickup he rode in the middle
So he'd never open a gate.

Conversin' with him was plum easy
He never had too much to say,
No matter what question you'd ask him
The answer was always, "Okay."

Well, they've lowered him down to the hard pan
And we've sung 'Shall we gather at'
They've asked for a moment of silence
And everyone's holdin' their hat.

Now the preacher is askin' me kindly
To say a few words at his death
So I mumble, and say, "He was steady . . . "
Then I pause and take a deep breath

But I'm too choked up to continue.
The crowd thinks I've been overcame
But the mason has screwed up his tombstone
And I can't remember his name!

14

Illustration: Bob Black

SIXTY FOOT ROPE

I was in Guadalajara, Mexico one time and ran into a man selling those long rawhide ropes, called them 'sogillas.' "How does
that work?" I asked. He built a loop tall as he was, threw a kind
of a hoolahan and caught a taco vendor on the other side!
"My gosh!" I said, "How long is that rope?'
"Catorce brazadas," he answered, 70 plus feet!

Most cowboys carry a 30 foot rope, 'cause that's a team ropin'
rope and you can buy them at the feed store second-hand for
$15! But, I have had the privilege of workin' with cowboys that
carry a 60 foot rope! Now, I never could figure out WHY they
would carry a 60' rope . . . maybe it's just because "I can!"

We were bringin' in a bunch of cows and calves to the big trap
with the intention of pullin' the calves off and takin' them to the
sale. I had two good cowboys helpin' me; Jack and Francisco.
There was one snakey black steer calf, weighed 525 lbs, I know
because he went to the sale next day! He kept quittin' the bunch
then finally shot right between me and Jack, right through my
good two-strand bobwire fence and took the bal-faced heifer and
the red high-horned cow with him!

Well, we were shippin'! We made chase through the gate into a
3-section pasture shakin' out our loops in hot pursuit! Jack took
after the heifer goin' north and Francisco went south through
the big arroyo and up the rocky ridge on the other side.

I could see the black steer runnin' the ridge line with Francisco
right behind him. That steer had his tail stickin' straight up
in the air, no lie, and the sun hung low on the winter morning
horizon and cast them in a silhouette. They looked like one of
those things they put over a driveway in Texas!

Francisco threw his loop, looked like he was crackin' a whip! That
rope settled down right over that steer's head...and MISSED! The
steer took a hard right into the arroyo and was headed my way.
Now, those of you cow people know that under the right conditions
a cow brute can increase his intellect to a sort-of primitive, reptilian, brain stem level. And a cowboy, like *moi*, can, under the
right conditions, i.e. done shook out a loop, he too can increase
his intellect to that same primitive, reptilian brain stem level!

They were made for each other, the cowboy and the cow, equals
in a love-hate relationship. There are analogies in real life; like
reporters and politicians. They hate each other but they can't
live without each other because each one wants to tell his side
of the story. And the ultimate analogy; lawyers and criminals!

16

You can see them talkin' to each other in front of the court-house and you wonder which one is which. I've decided how to tell the difference; if he's a good lawyer the criminal is always wearing a better suit!

So there I sat on the lip of the arroyo, on the trail comin' out, got a loop shook out on my 30' rope and my horse can sense the excitement, too. It's like we're backin' up in the box...we're standing on six tip toes!

That steer came out of that arroyo like a dirt bike comin' out of a jump! For a microsecond our eyes met and we became one. It's like becoming one with a creosote post, or a railroad tie. I could see him lookin' this way, then that way, but when he made up his mind I could tell...he came straight for me!

My immediate reaction was to throw my loop as he shot by me at the speed of beef! I caught! I'm throwin' my dallies and he's jerkin'em out of my hand fast as I can throw'em! Finally he took the whole rope out of my hand, thank goodness, or I'da been flipped over backwards and killed . . . and somebody else would be writing this book!

Ten minutes later I am down on my hands and knees in the bottom of that arroyo with the hot sun on my back and the vicious thorns tearing at my clothing, and holding onto this horse who would go home if I let him and I could never get within two feet of that rope!

Then, like Saul on the road to Damascus, the light shone down upon me and I said, "This is why they carry a 60' rope!"

Illustration: Dave Holl

17

COWBOY TIME

If Genesis was right on track concerning Adam's birth
And seven days was all it took to build the planet Earth,
Then where does carbon dating fit? And all the dinosaurs?
Plus all that other ancient stuff that happened on our shores?

Now, I believe in scientists. They aren't just lunatics!
But I believe in Genesis, which leaves me in a fix.
The answer finally came to me while making up this rhyme,
God made the earth in seven days
but that was Cowboy Time . . .

Have you ever called the shoer to set aside a day
You scrutinize your calendar, say "Tuesday'd be okay."
The big day comes, you take off work, alas, he's never seen.
You call him back and he inquires,
"Which Tuesday did you mean?"

Did you ever place an order to get a saddle made?
An A-Fork tree and padded seat with silver hand-inlaid.
As decades pass, all you can do is sit around and eat
So by the time it finally comes you've padded your own seat!

A friend came by on July 4th. He swore he couldn't stay
But then he said, "For just a bit." He left on Christmas Day!
'A couple days, a little while, not long, or right away!'
Should not be taken literally in cowboyville today.

But like I said, the precedent was set so long ago.
The angels had to learn themselves what all good cowboys know.
They worried if they didn't work to keep the schedule tight
That Earth would not be finished by the deadline Sunday night.

They'd never really thought in terms of rollin' with the flow
But God does things in Cowboy Time . . .
to watch the flowers grow.
He bade the angels to relax and said, "For Heaven's sakes,
I'll get it done in seven days . . . however long it takes!"

18

A COWFUL

Grandpa Tommy's dad used to say "A cowful is a great sufficiency." According to my research, the rumen on a mature cow can hold up to 300 pounds. And by anybody's standards that is a substantial quantity.

Say you had a cowful of pocket change. You'd almost need a cow to keep it in. Say you had a cowful of wet laundry. It would take a forklift to get it in the dryer. Say you had a cowful of manure. Well, I guess a lot of us do.

If cowful became an accepted unit of measure it could replace the antiquated English standards like the dram and the rod. And those bland, simple minded metric names that somehow sound communistic; kiloliter, hectometer, decigram. Can you picture in your mind a decigram? Is it the weight of a decimated graham cracker? Or ten grandmas standin' on the scale?

Under the cowful system 15 scoopfuls would equal a cowful. Two bootfuls would make a scoopful, two hatfuls would make a bootful. Half a hatful would equal a capful.

6 canfuls, as in beer cans, makes a capful. One canful equals 40 thimblefuls, 20 teardrops in a thimbleful.

The dosage for penicillin would read: 4 teardrops per 5 scoopfuls of body weight IM.

For Blackleg four-way vaccination: 1 thimbleful SQ. Repeat in 60 days.

Bizarre, you say. If cowful was a measure of weight or volume, possibly the distance between postholes would become the standard unit of measure for length, i.e. 660 postholes per section line - 4 thumbs to a hand, 3 hands to a foot, 4 feet to a coyote length and 2 coyote lengths to a posthole.

Decibels of loudness would be described in more understandable terms. From chicken peck to pig squeal for everyday sounds. Loud noises would be categorized as small wreck, big wreck and heck'uva wreck.

"So, did you hear about Orb gettin bucked off? Must'a sailed 5 coyote lengths, hit the side of the grain bin with a moose bugle and two cowfuls of pellets fell on him. Smashed him flatter'n a rabbit ear.

"They got him to the Doc in half a coon's age, transfused him with a six pack of type 0 negative and removed a posthole of intestine. He's doin' okay but he's lost about six hatfuls.

"He's been a sheep's gestation recovering. Doc says it's shock, but I figger it just scared a pea waddin' and a half out of him. Well, I gotta go. I've got an appointment in 4 1/2 shakes of a lamb's tail."

ଓ

DRESSIN' UP

Dressin' up to certain good folks
Might mean a suit and a tie
Designer socks, a diamond ring
Or hair like the Fourth of July!

But out where we make a livin'
Tennis shoes don't fit the bill.
They don't set too good in a stirrup.
I reckon they never will.

We're more into spurs, hats and leggin's
'Cause punchin' cows ain't all romance
But cowboys clean up on occasion
For weddings, a funeral or dance.

The dress code for everyday cowboys
Ain't changed since Grandpa got wise,
A good pair of boots, a scarf if it's clean
And yer newest pair of blue jeans.

Besides, deckin' a cowboy out
In street shoes, a suit and a tie
Would make as good an impression
As croutons on a cow pie.

FIXIN' THE OUTHOUSE

The ol' man wuz layin' there on the sofa and the ol' lady come in and said, "Get out there and fix that outhouse!"

The ol' man got up and ambled out and hammered a few nails and come back in and laid down. Here she come!

"I thought I told you to git out there and fix that outhouse!" He snapped offa there a little quicker. He went out and hammered that piece of tin that had been flappin' all winter and he come back in and laid down. Here she come!

"You sorry ol' buzzard! If you don't get out there and fix that outhouse I'm gonna slap you into next week!"

He come offa there like a rocket! He run out to the shop and got his tools. He got his shovel and went around the foundation; hammered every nail in and set it! He took them little pieces of tar and patched that tin roof. He tightened that hinge up and greased 'er, he went over that sucker with a fine tooth comb! She come out to see what wuz takin' him so long.

He was givin' it such a thorough inspection. He had his head down inside the hole, peerin' around...

She spooked him!

He jerked his head outta that hole and caught his chin whiskers in a crack in the lip of the seat right there!

"Dadgummit!" he said.

She said, "Aggrivatin', ain't it?"

GRANDPA'S WISDOM OF THE AGES

Grandpas have a special job and have since days of yore
To teach his children's children things his parents might ignore.
Like how to spit and whistle, carve initials on a tree
The value of an empty can and why some things aren't free.

Why dogs get stuck, how birds can fly,
why Grandma's always right
And how to tie a square knot and the time to stand and fight.
And, if Grandpa's a cowboy and the kid is so inclined
The horn of wisdom empties out to fill his little mind.

He has the kid upon a horse as soon as Mom allows
And fills him full of stories 'bout the old days punchin' cows.
And how when he was "just your age"
he rode the rough string snides
And never hesitated, see, that's how he learned how to ride.

So when the horse the kid was ridin' tossed him to the ground
The Grandpa said, "Now get back on,
don't let him keep you down."
The boy balked but Grandpa knew the lesson to be learned
"One of us must ride this horse," he said, his voice stern.

Then wisdom passed from old to young,
"Yer right," the kid said true,
"You want I let the stirrups out . . . just one hole or two?"

23

COWBOY BRIDE

All the usual suspects were lined up behind the groom.
The smell of cheap tequila rose from their side of the room.
They looked like boneless chickens,
plucked and feelin' none too good,
All the victims of the night before's farewell to bachelorhood.

The bride was making mental notes to have the best man flogged,
To doublecheck the ladies room that earlier had clogged,
Regretting that the rented tuxes weren't a better fit
And hoping that the photographs would not show up her zit.

The preacher opened up his Book
and beamed a practiced smile,
"We are gathered here together....get that kid out of the aisle!
He's standing on your train and
leaving chocolate finger marks!"
She turned and hissed, "Git off my dress
or I'll feed you to the sharks!"

The kid jumped off the wrinkled train - but sister filled the gap
She grabbed the end and gave it one good
'change the sheets' type snap.
The whole thing came off in her hands!
The bride, once fully dressed,
From thong to slippers now was bared to the assembled guests.

Just then the bridesmaid groaned
and ran back toward the potted plants.
The bug-eyed preacher stopped and stared,
then cast his eyes askance.
"It's morning sickness," said the bride,
"She's gonna have to blow.
I've got it, too," she whispered,
"So just get on with the show."

"The ring?" The preacher asked the groom.
But he was in a trance.
The best man nudged him gently,
then reached down in his pants,
"My pocket's got a hole in it!
The ring's gone down to my boot!"
"Well, get it out!" the bride replied,
"I'm not too proud to shoot."

In stocking foot the best man
helped the groom present the ring.
The bridesmaid in her spotted dress stood by encouraging.
But when they went to place the ring upon the groom's left hand,
He keeled over backwards knocking out the poor best man.

The new bride caught the preacher's eye...
Impaled him with a glare,
"He does," she said, "And so do I." Her challenge filled the air.
"Then I pronounce you man and wife . . . Let nothing gang aglay.
I wish you all the very best . . . you may drag the groom away."

Some might think this cowboy marriage
was ordained an early death.
But friends, if you had seen her . . .
not as long as she drew breath.

She just threw him in the pickup,
popped the clutch
and waved goodbye
With the dog up front
beside her, lookin' life
right in the eye.

Illustration: Don Gill

JUNIOR

Now, Junior is tough and can't git enough
of lively confrontations
And bein' his friend, I'm asked to defend
his slight miscalculations.

Among his mistakes, too often he makes
none of his business . . . his.
So I counsel restraint 'cause sometimes he ain't
as tough as he *thinks* he is!

Like the time he cut loose in a bar called the Moose
in Dillon on rodeo night.
I stayed on his tail in hopes to prevail
and maybe prevent us a fight

But Junior's headstrong and it didn't take long
'til he got in a debate
Involving a chair and big hunks of hair
and startin' to obligate

His friends, I could see, which only was me!
A fact I couldn't ignore,
So takin' his arm to lead him from harm
I drug my pal to the door.

No one disagreed and I thought that we'd
made our escape free and clear
But he turned to the crowd and said good and loud,
"Who is the toughest guy here!"

Not the smartest remark in a place this dark,
ol' Junior had gone too far!
No one said a word, but I knew they heard
'cause all heads turned to the bar

And there in the hole like a power pole
stood the pressure for all his peers.
"Ugly for Hire" and he wore a truck tire
that came down over his ears!

He had on some chaps with big rubber straps
but over his arms instead!
And sported a pattern like the planet Saturn
his eyebrows went clear round his head!

His good eye glared while his nostrils flared
like a winded Lippizan
Which lent him the air of a wounded bear
whose pointer'd been stepped upon!

A Crescent wrench swung from where it hung
on a log chain wrapped round his neck,
Along with a claw, a circular saw
and parts from a Harley wreck!

With his Sumo girt he needed no shirt.
Shoot, he had no place to tuck it!
And wonders don't cease, he wore a codpiece
made from a backhoe bucket!

He was Fantasyland, the Marlboro Man
and heartburn all rolled into one!
From where I was lookin' our goose was cookin',
our cowboy days were done!

Then he spoke from the hole like a thunder roll
that came from under the sea.
He swallowed his snuff . . . said, "If yer huntin' tough,
I reckon that'ud be me."

I heard a pin drop. The clock even stopped!
Silence . . . 'cept for me heavin'.
But Junior, instead, just pointed and said,
"*You! Take over, we're leavin'!*"

COWBOYS ADVICE TO THE LOVELORN

The Ventura County Star carried an advice column written by three cowboys. They inspired me.

DEAR SADDLE TRIO, My wife wants a divorce but still insists on us going to a marriage counselor, so she can say she tried. What should I do? SIGNED, IN-THE-CROSSHAIRS

DEAR CROSSHAIRS - Change states.

DEAR TRIPLE TIE-DOWN TRIAD, I'm a 22 year-old ex-model, now bank Vice-President with a new Dodge dually, 3 horse slant, ranchette with roping arena, and 4 credit cards. How can I get my surfing boyfriend to pop the question? SIGNED, PALOMINO YEARNING

DEAR YEARNING - Kiss your surfing smoothie goodbye, and send a copy of your resume, complete with a picture of the Dodge dually to: thetritipcowboys@rightonbaby.com

DEAR TUMBLEWEED TRIAGE, Our first wedding anniversary is coming up soon and I'd like to get a gift for my wonderful cowboy hubby that will be thoughtful, sweet and demonstrative of my love for him that will last through the ages.
SIGNED, STILL SWOONING

DEAR SWOONING - Beer is always a good choice.

DEAR TRIPE-EATING TRIPLETS, I'd like to marry my cowboy, Robert, and have proposed to him in a poem, which I can't quite finish. Can you help me? It begins:
"I'll marry you, I'm ready, Bob,
If you'll just get a steady ..." SIGNED, ANXIOUS IN OXNARD

DEAR ANXIOUS - Sorry; nothing comes to mind.

DEAR TRIANGULAR TRAILRIDERS, My cowboy has been out in the wagon and I haven't seen him for six weeks. Any ideas for what I might wear for our first night back together? SIGNED, STARS IN HER EYES

DEAR STARS - Barbecue sauce

DEAR TRUCULENT TAPADERAS, My live-in boyfriend is starting to make eyes at other women. The other love of my life is a hard-to-handle Arabian stallion. I realize I can't afford them both. What should I do? SIGNED, PUZZLED IN PIOCHE

DEAR PUZZLED - Flip a coin and geld the one you keep.

DEAR 3 DIMENSIONAL TROUBADORS, I'm courting a shiny lookin' dolly who wants to get married. But she's been engaged to half the men in Modesto. Should that concern me? SIGNED, RELUCTANT ROUSER

DEAR RELUCK - Shiny's always good. Besides, Modesto ain't that big.

DEAR TROUBLESOME TRIFECTA, I met a woman in Sturgis at the Rally. She has a motorcycle and a tattoo. We're getting serious, but I don't want to play second fiddle to her cycle passion. Is she a good bet? SIGNED, IDLING IN IDAHO

DEAR IDS - It depends. Is it a Harley? . . . the tattoo, I mean?

DEAR TRIPLICATING COWPUNCHERS, What's the best way to get a guy to commit? SIGNED, DESPERATELY SEEKING

DEAR DESPERATELY - Commit to what?

THE BOAT ROPING

If God intended cows to swim, He'd given them all flippers.
You rarely see a mermaid calf or Holstein skinny dippers.
But in their battle to survive, I've seen cows come unraveled
And to escape the cowboy's loop will choose the path less traveled.

Now Randy wasn't brilliant but he was a heavy breather,
Which helps when chasing wild cows
who aren't that brilliant either.
To try and even up the odds he called his neighbor Steven
One cow versus two cowboys intellectually's 'bout even.

The cow in question spotted them, stuck her tail in the air
And lit out for a tank dam in the pasture yonder there.
Randy fell in hot pursuit whilst shakin' a big loop out.
He knew he had to catch her quick
or his horse and him would poop out.

She led him round the tank dam circumnavigating right
So Steve went round the other way to cut her off in flight.
Please picture if you will the scene,
two jousting knights converging,
A loco'd cow between the two, collision courses merging.

She hit the bank, took one big leap and dove in like a porpoise.
The last thing our two cowboys saw was a disappearing orifice.
She swam out to the middle
where her feet could still touch bottom,
Submerged there in the water looking vaguely hippopottom.

"We've got her now!" cried Randy as he bailed off his hoss,
And jumped into a rowboat that was tethered in the moss.
He grabbed an oar and cast away and started paddling wildly
And rowed himself out toward the cow
who watched him crocodildly.

He roped her off the starboard
and half hitched her to the bowsprit.
But . . . she breached just like a marlin and covered him with . . .
Sorry, I couldn't come up with a rhyme for bowsprit.

He planned to tow her backwards
but her feet dug in the sea floor
And pulled him clear across the pond
and out upon the lee shore.

"Abandon ship, you lunatic!" Steve yelled above the racket.
"I can't!" he cried, "I left my life vest in my other jacket!"
The hull was flyin' all apart, and headed for a shipwreck,
The poop deck lived up to its name,
or should that be cow-chip-deck?

Great big pieces crashed and cratered
scaring fish and water fowl.
Seals barked, catfish mewed, I even heard an otter growl.
But he hung on there behind the cow
despite the flying shrapnel,
No doubt to go down with his ship like any good ship cap'n'l.

Long story short Steve's horse rebelled
and pitched him where it's stickery.
He watched the cow and rowboat disappearing in the hickory
With Randy still connected like the tail of a comet
Most probably feeling seasick
but without the time to think about it.

A piece of keel between two oak trees
snagged'em like an anchor,
Stopped'em like a hangman's rope,
capsized the ship and sank'er.
The cow had Randy up a tree, up there in all his glory
As she butted up against the trunk and marked her territory.

"Pretty scary," hollered Stevo,
"I'm surprised you wasn't drownded!"
"That cow just plain outfoxed me,"
muttered Randy, then expounded
"But . . . I've learned myself a lesson, a basic rule refresher,
That cow, the boat, and me can't hold our water under pressure!

31

AARP!

Of late there's been a modest debate
involving the wearing of fur.
There's some even swears
anybody who wears it is flawed in their character.
Yet others will fight to maintain their right
to wear what they dang well please
But the answer lies in a compromise
that sets both minds at ease.

Imagine two friends at opposite ends
who meet and do lunch once a week.
Their friendship is tried when they gather outside
a Beverly Hills boutique.
"Sylvia, oh my soul, is that a mink stole?
Please tell me it's fake from Goodwill!"
"Yes, Babs, it is mink, but it's not what you think,
because...it's designer roadkill!"

Oh, sure, you scoff, but don't blow it off
it's the wisdom of Solomon's voice.
The perfect solution, it grants absolution
yet leaves the owner Pro Choice!
Wisdom so pure should forever endure
and percolate into your soul
So I'm the head jack of the Animal Accident Recovery Patrol!

The AARP! Which is Larry and me, are on the road every night
To gently remind you that mess left behind you
is more than a buzzard's delight!
Carry your trowel for mammal or fowl
to collect your vehicular blooper.
In time you will find yucky's all in your mind,
no worse than a pooper scooper!

Plus, you'll be amazed how activists praise you
for doin' what you think is right
And no trapper'd object if you stopped to collect
things that go bump in the night.
But treat it with care, waste not a hare,
be sorry, but don't sit and pine,
'Cause accidents happen when yer both overlappin'
the double yellow line.

So salvage your plunder and render your blunder
into a warm winter coat
And remember our motto as you know you otto it follows,
and herein I quote,
"MAKE IT A HABIT TO PICK UP YOUR RABBIT
DON'T LEAVE HIM TO DRY IN THE SUN
FOR THE SAKE OF A GARMENT, RECYCLE YOUR VARMINT
IT'S TACKY TO JUST HIT AND RUN!"

Illustration: Baxter Black

WORKIN' FOR WAGES

I've worked fer wages all my life
watchin' other people's stock
And the outfits I hired on to
didn't make you punch the clock

Let you work until you finished!
Like the feedlots in the fall,
When they'd roll them calves in on ya
they'd jis' walk the fence and bawl.

We'd check the pens and pull the sick
and push and treat and ride
Then process new arrivals
that kept comin' like the tide.

And I've calved a lotta heifers
though it's miserable sometimes,
It's something that I'm good at
and it's like she's sorta mine.

She knows I ain't the owner
but we're not into protocol.
She's a cow and I'm a cowboy
and I guess that says it all . . .

Got no truck with politicians
who whine and criticize
'Bout corporate agribusiness,
I guess they don't realize

Somebody's gotta own 'em
that can pay the entry fee!
Why, who they think puts up the dough
to hire ol' boys like me?

Oh, I bought a set of heifers once
maybe fifteen years ago.
I had 'em through a calvin'
then I had to let 'em go.

'Cause all I did was worry
'bout how to pay the bills.
Took the fun outta cow punchin'.
I don't need them kinda thrills.

Though I wouldn't mind a'ownin' me
a little hideaway
So when some outfit laid me off
I'd have a place to stay

But I figger I'm jis' lucky
to be satisfied at heart
That I'm doin' what I'm good at
and I'm playin' a small part

In a world that's complicated,
where the bosses fight it out
With computers and consultants
and their counterparts with clout.

They're so busy bein' bosses,
they've no time to spare, somehow,
So they have to hire someone like me
to go out and punch their cow.

LEBKUCHENS ON THE TRAIL

Every Christmas, as regular as an insulin shot we receive one of my favorite annual gifts. 16 square feet of Lebkuchens. My mother-in-law manufactures these unusual cookies in her garage or possibly in her metallurgy studio. I've never asked about the recipe or the cooking directions.

I assume she uses a cement mixer, pours the sticky dough out on the driveway to dry. It thickens in the sun, then is rolled flat by the kids next door. Once it has hardened it can be lifted like a sheet of plywood and allowed to age like fine wine, silage or Chinese 1,000-year eggs. Since she has no cellar, the sheets of dough are stacked like lumber behind the shop under a blue tarp.

Time goes by. It is a secret how long the dough is allowed to molder, compress, steep, cure, condense and heal but I have seen newspapers stuck to the bottom with President Nixon's picture. I saw the initials BB carved in one like you would put your handprint in cement. I guessed it was Buffalo Bill's.

At harvest time you have a foodstuff that is impervious to toxic chemicals, boiling or radiation, the denseness of an anvil, has the half-life of a radial tire and smells vaguely like licorice and Easy Off. I have seen the table saw she uses to cut them into 2x3 inch squares. It has a 10" masonry blade.

Of course, it is not always wise to examine the process. Like making sausage or legislation, making Lebkuchens is messy. But the result is an addictive, delicious, filling, chewy, long-lasting, floss-proof delicacy you can carry in your back pocket like a wallet, or in your saddlebags.

In addition to lasting longer than jerky, plastic bottles in a landfill, or 7% iodine on your fingers, it can be molded into decorative or functional shapes to shim your welding table, resole shoes, or patch a pinkeye.

Lebkuchens crossed the Bearing Strait with Strom Thurmond, climbed the North Pole with Admiral Perry and were used as a heat shield on Apollo 13.

So, you can see why I wait every year for my Lebkuchens to arrive. They are the cowboy's ultimate tool, to pave with, to sharpen your knife on, to pad your saddle, shoe your horse, scrape unsightly scurf off your elbows and heels, and you can eat them!

My favorite Frederic Remington painting features a cowboy holding the all-purpose snack aloft as if saluting. It's called simply, "Lebkuchens on the Trail."

TISSUE ON THE RANGE

Sheryl Crow, popular pop singer, made headlines in 2007 by proposing a method to waste less natural resources. It made us cowboys look environmentally ahead of our time.

A purist global warming star said we should use less paper
When tending to hygienic needs, we should begin to taper
Our use of trees and bark and pulp, in forests do not linger
Restrict yourself to one small sheet . . .
and use your index finger!
It soon became a global joke although it lit the issue
But, in hind sight, forgive the pun, cowboys rarely see a tissue!

To prove my point take western art replete with cowboy wrecks
In landscapes big and beautiful. Were there any bright white flecks
Of paper in the sagebrush or adorning roundup scenes?
Did Russell edit them all out or were cowboys so dang clean
They never littered! Not even once? Now, that, I strongly doubt.
They used what was available. The practical way out.

Which wasn't always pretty. Some things are rough and coarse
Like willer limbs, ya hold the ends and drag it back and forth.
Or pine tree boughs to scoot along, all sticky drippin' sap
Or shirttails, accidentally, or the fringes on your chaps.
Dakotans got their wheat straw, Coloradans, cockleburs,
Californians use exotic fruits that come in his and hers.

Wyoming and Montana claim that sheep can oft suffice
A farmer up in Utah says you can use a seagull twice!
Indians wore a loincloth as their chosen mode of dress
The front, to guard their modesty, the hind, well you can guess.

Oh, how I envy cowboys who live where there are trees
'Cause 'mongst the brush and prickly pear
there dang sure ain't no leaves!
I've been reduced to horny toads and jagged sun-baked rocks,
But there's been times, desperate times,
I rode home with no socks.

And yes, I've used tortillas that I've found along the trail
Or rummaged in my pocket for a baby cottontail.
Almost anything you'd think of, a cowboy's prob'ly tried
Though bob wire fence and icicles might be hard to stay astride.

We should give them carbon credits
'cause the western artists show
They leave no sign of paper sheets or Charmin in the snow
So, we tip our hat to cowboys who deserve to get their due
And be recognized as number one in the art of number two!

38

THE OYSTER

The sign upon the cafe wall said OYSTERS: fifty cents.
"How quaint," the blue-eyed sweetheart said
with some bewildermence,
"I didn't know they served such fare out here upon the plain."
"Oh, sure," her cowboy date replied,
"We're really quite urbane."

*"I would guess they're Chesapeake or Blue Point,
don't you think?"*
"No ma'am, they're mostly Hereford cross...
and usually they're pink
But I've been cold, so cold myself, what you say could be true
And if a man looked close enough,
their points could sure be blue!"

She said, *"I gather them myself out on the bay alone.
I pluck them from the murky depths
and smash them with a stone!"*
The cowboy winced, imagining a calf with her beneath,
"Me, I use a pocket knife and yank'em with my teeth."

"Oh my," she said, *"You animal! How crude and unrefined!
Your masculine assertiveness sends shivers up my spine!
But I prefer a butcher knife too dull to really cut,
I wedge it in on either side and crack it like a nut!*

*I pry them out. If they resist, sometimes I use the pliers
Or even Grandpa's pruning shears if that's what it requires!"*
The hair stood on the cowboy's neck.
His stomach did a whirl.
He'd never heard such grisly talk, especially from a girl!

"I like them fresh," the sweetheart said
and laid her menu down
Then ordered oysters for them both
when the waiter came around.

The cowboy smiled gamely,
though her words stuck in his craw
But he finally fainted dead away
when she said, *"I'll have mine raw!"*

THE REAL THING

He was lookin' for work. I was buildin' corrals, stretchin' wire, layin' rock and clearin' brush. I asked him what he could do. He said, "I'm a cowboy." For six months Frank built corrals, stretched wire, laid rock and cleared brush. He worked hard and stayed on. It was skilled labor but hard on the back and hands.

Last spring I went to Gerald's branding and asked him if I could bring along an extra hand. Gerald said the more the merrier. "Can he ride?" he asked. "Well," I replied, "He told me he was a cowboy."

We got to the ranch and Gerald got him mounted. Frank had brought an old rope but no chaps or spurs. We rode out to gather the bunch. Gerald asked me if I'd drag calves to the fire since we were short-handed. Flattered, I said, "You bet." By mid-morning we'd gathered a hundred or so cows with calves into a tight trap.

On Gerald's orders we were trying to sort out a big high horned half Bramer barren cow. Four times we got her to the gate and four times she broke back. Gerald was determined, and he *is* a good cowboy. He roped her and started draggin' her toward the gate. She went down. Wouldn't budge. Stuck like a D-8 Cat in a cranberry bog.

"Git another rope on her," Gerald hollered. While I was fumblin' around tryin' to unleash my rope I saw a beautiful flat loop sail over my horse's nose from left to right and settle around the cow's butt. Frank's rope came tight. One hard pull and she was on her feet and the two of thcm drug her out the gate. The dynamics of our little group changed perceptively.

Thirty minutes later we had 'em in the branding corral. All but one 200 pound black bally calf. Wild as a deer, it took us several tries to get him back up to the fence but he couldn't find the gate. Gerald eased up to within ten feet, threw an easy loop...and missed. The calf spun like an Olympic swimmer and shot between us. I heard a whiz and a whoosh. Frank had thrown his rope from a sideways position, fired it like a harpoon and caught that calf goin' straight away on a dead run at twenty feet.

Gerald looked at me, "I b'lieve I'll ask Frank if he'll drag 'em to the fire." "It would be the right thing," I said, with a new found respect we both felt.

Frank, whose real name is Francisco, is still punchin' cows, buildin' fence and settin' posts for me. There's lots of Franks and Franciscos and Bobbys, Josés, Eddies and Rogers out there sellin' feed, teachin' school, drivin' trucks and pickin' strawberries. Drawin' a paycheck.

That's what they do, but it's not what they are. If you ask 'em, they'll look you straight in the eye and tell ya, "Soy un vaquero . . . I'm a cowboy."

Illustration: Dave Holl

41

THE EPITAPH

That ol' man could sure set a post. Three foot down
in the hardest ground,
grunt and thud, chink and chime.
Bedrock trembled beneath his bar. Each new whack
broke the back of granite old as time.

Be easier to move it. The hole, that is.
But that wasn't his way of settin' a post.
His ran like a soldier's backbone, straight as a die
to the naked eye. Perfect . . . not just close.

He'd scoop the dirt into it in a careful way.
Like sculptor's clay he'd add an inch or two.
"Each one counts," he'd say to me, then tamp that thing
'til the bar would ring and the earth was black and blue.

He set cedar and steel but what he liked most
was an eight foot post, the butt of a telephone pole.
Called it 'plantin' a deadman' for bobwire fence
to stretch against. Made a heck'uva hole!

Big enough to bury a dog! Speakin' of which,
last week he pitched straight over face down and died.
Not buildin' fence like you might think but on his knees
tendin' trees that grew on the windbreak side.

For twenty years we neighbored well, which just makes sense,
our common fence was always strong and tight.
But, Lord, he did things the hard way! Flat wore me out!
But I don't doubt he tried to do 'em right!

They struggled for an epitaph to consecrate,
in words ornate, the place they'd lay his head.
They didn't ask me. I weren't no kin to the lad
but if they had, this is what I'd say,

"He could sure set a post." One man's stand
in the shifting sand of the world as it is today
That offered hope. An anchor, dug in deep,
that helped to keep us all from driftin' away.

CHAPTER 2
COW, CALF,
RANCHING

This phase of the cattle business involves pure-bred and commercial breeders.

The purebred breeders are the architects who design prototypes for the industry. They are academic minded. They steep themselves in statistics, fiddle with and refine genetics in an effort to define subjective traits, objectively. It in not unlike ancient mariners drawing and redrawing the constellations in the night sky.

The commercial cow/calf operators are the bedrock of the industry, the worker on the assembly line. They produce our product, beef, from scratch just as a welder builds a bumper guard, a cook bakes an apple pie, or an artist paints a picture.

They think in terms of generations (both human and bovine), take the good with the bad and have a loyalty to the land. You rarely hear one say, "I'm just ranchin' long enough make the money to buy a car dealership downtown."

This group is a bountiful source of cowboy stories. I think it is because, so often, it is one cowboy versus one cow. It pits two equals in constant conflict. I would suggest God put them in his plan when He was seeking to add some humor to the vast universe.

THE COW COMMITTEE

Once upon a time at the start of all creation
Angels sat upon a cloud. An odd conglomeration
Of buckaroos from near and far but not there from the city.
Their job; to build a brand new beast.
They were the Cow Committee.

"Now me, I'd like some floppy ears," suggested Texas Jake.
"Floppy ears would freeze plum off on the Powder or the Snake!"
"Up north we need some curly hair," said Colorado Bill,
"Hide that's tight and hair that's thick to ward against the chill."

"Hold yer horses, one and all," said Omaha Eugene,
"Nebraska needs a fleshy cow; a real corn machine!"
"She'd waste away!" cried Tucson Bob, "What we need's a hump.
One who'll live on tumbleweeds and run from clump to clump."

"How 'bout horns?" said Oakdale Pete.
"Don't need'em in Des Moines."
"We'll make some with and some without
and some with tenderloins."
"Some with sheaths that drag the grass and some so dadgum tall
To hear her calf down on the ground she'd have to place a call!"

"I'd like'm roan," said Shorthorn Mike.
"No, black," said Angus Tink.
"White or red," said Hereford Hank, "I'd even take'm pink!"
"Whatever suits you tickles me," said Juan from Mexico.
"I second that," said Crossbred Jack,
"Just make'm so they grow."

They made some white. They made some blue.
They made some orange and spotted.
They never made a green one but they made'm tall and squatted.
In every shape and every size but no one had decided
How to make the perfect cow; on that they were divided.

This went on for days and days, in fact, it never ended.
Each time they reached some middle ground
the project was amended.
They still meet from time to time and argue with their leaders.
The Cow Committee carries on...
they're now the purebred breeders.

Illustration: Charlie Marsh

BENTLEY THE BORN-AGAIN BULL

It was one of those two o'clock mornin' calls: "Looked like everything was comin' jes fine, Doc, then he got stuck! Could you come?"

On the way out to the ranch I put the truck on autopilot while my foggy brain sifted through the possibilities. Hip lock, more than likely, I figgered. I walked into the calvin' barn, shook the snow off my coat and surveyed the scene. Fairly peaceful. Two unshaven cowboys playin' cards in front of the space heater and a good-sized heifer standing in the chute looking no worse for the wear. "Good," I thought, "The boys haven't worn the heifer out before they called." Or themselves either, for that matter.

I peeled down to my shortsleeve coveralls and went to survey the battlefield. There, underneath the heifer's cocked tail, peering out at the new world was Bentley, the baby bull calf. All I could see was his head. With mama's help he'd gotten far enough to pop his nose and his ears out and no further. He didn't seem in distress, just a little embarrassed. He looked like some trophy hunter's prize hangin' on the den wall.

Since the umbilical cord hadn't broken yet he had no need to breathe but he was lookin' around like a kid in a neck brace at the county fair. After my examination I concluded he had one front leg into the birth canal and the other pointing straight back. He was wedged in tight as a new hat band.

"Bentley," I said, "I hope you brought your scuba gear because you've got to go back inside." I gave the heifer an epidural injection so she couldn't strain. I put my hand over his nose and started to push. Bentley raised an eyebrow and looked up at me. "You sure you've got a license to do this?" he said. "Sure," says I, "I bought it from a guy in Iowa when he sold out his practice!"

It wasn't easy, but I popped the little duffer back in, straightened his legs and then pulled him into the outside world.

He was typically ungrateful as I rubbed him down and pointed him to the breakfast nook under mama's flank. He turned once and looked at me, "I've heard of being born again," he said, "but this is ridiculous!"

46

SHE DOES THE BOOKS

This is my wife. She does the books
I do the important stuff
Like mend the fence and check the cows,
She makes sure the income's enough

To cover the cost of farmin'.
She's tight as a new hat band.
I need to buy a new baler,
She figgers out if we can.

I spend all day in the pickup,
She's in the office all day
Just talkin' with the SCS
Or checkin' the price of hay

Or dealin' with the accountants
And keepin' the banker straight
I might be cleanin' a ditch out
Or hangin' a rusty gate

She fills out all the blasted forms
The government makes us keep.
She reads those regulations till
She's fightin'em in her sleep.

Me, I go to sleep a'dreamin'
Of bulls and barns and sales,
She's dreamin' the inventory
Or estimatin' bales.

She still finds time to bake a pie
Between her business deals
And I keep busy all the time
Just greasin' squeaky wheels.

I told my wife that we should think
'Bout gettin' a hired man.
Runnin' a farm ain't easy,
Good managers need a plan.

She agreed that it weren't easy
To manage and keep abreast
"But, why," she asked, "Get a hired man?
I've already got the best."

EVOLUTION OF THE RANCH WIFE

October,   (NEWLYWEDS)
"Honey, the boys and I will be workin' cows all day. It's dangerous and dirty, especially for a pretty little thing like you. We'll be up to the house at noon. I'd sure appreciate it if you could fix us some lunch. There'll only be five of us but if you need help don't hesitate to call my mother."

April,   (MARRIED 3 YEARS)
"Emily Jean, you stand behind that barrel. Sometimes these heifers get feisty after they calve. Once I get her tied down you hand me those chains and the calf puller. Be careful, Darlin', it's heavy."

July,   (MARRIED 6 YEARS)
"Emily, sugar, the hayin' crew will be in at lunch time. I think there's 12 of 'em. I don't wanna stop this mornin' so when you bring out the coffee and sweet rolls at 9:30 would you mind just catchin' up to each baler and give it to the driver on the run. By the way, the tax man will be here at one o'clock. Take care of him, will ya?"

November,   (MARRIED 10 YEARS)
"Emily, you sure you got that chain hooked good enough? Let the clutch out easy. When you feel the tractor starting to lug, drop to a lower gear and go slow. I don't want to lose any bales off the back of the pickup. Just follow the tracks. When we get out to the cows, I'll trade you. You can toss the bales and I'll drive. You wanna borrow my slicker?"

September,   (MARRIED 13 YEARS)
"Em, crawl under here and hold this nut. I'll get up under the hood and turn the bolt from above. Watch out for that grease spot."

May,   (MARRIED 17 YEARS)
"Mother, you spray the fly dope and keep the blackleg gun full. I'll rope'm. Junior and Jenny can help you flank the big calves."

October,   (MARRIED A LONG TIME)
"Ma, we're runnin' outta cows! Push'em up!"

March,   (NOT LONG AGO)
"Dang it, I checked the heifers at midnight. It's yore turn."

THE PHONE CALL

It's always been a myst'ry in the winter when it's slow
Why a rancher gets up early when he's got no place to go!

He prowls around the kitchen like a burglar on parole
In his air-conditioned slippers with the toe there in the hole.

Then he builds a pot of coffee and has a little cup
'Til he thinks of some good reason to wake somebody up!

And all around the valley folks are nestled in their bed
Unaware an egg is hatching in the rancher's little head.

He's reread the livestock paper since getting up alone
But he's still not quite decided just who he's gonna phone!

The assistant county agent? The forest ranger's boss?
The banker? Brand inspector? The commissioner that lost?

The vet? The Co-op salesman? Though he can't recall his name,
But it really doesn't matter 'cause anybody's game.

He quivers like a panther about to pounce his prey
As the innocent lay sleeping just a dial tone away.

By daylight it's all over and he's reached a fever pitch!
The way he's stompin' 'round the house his wife is wond'rin' which

Potential victim got the call and had his brain massaged
With the lecture, she, just yesterday, herself, had tried to dodge!

But little does she realize just why he's in a tizzy,
See, his neighbors got up earlier . . . and all the lines were busy!

THE DEAD COW RANCH

Bubba and Billy Bob grew up together. From grade school on. They's best of friends. Now Billy Bob was one of them fellers who had the "King Midas touch." Everything he touched turned to gold. Bubba, on the other hand; everything he touched turned to sheep pellets! Billy Bob was the class valedictorian, captain of the football team and Twirp King. Bubba never graduated.

Well, they both went into the cow business and married up. Billy Bob's success continued. He paid off the loan the first year on his cows. In five years he owned his place free and clear. To this day Bubba has NEVER owned a cow free and clear! Matter of fact, in 1993 Bubba changed the name of his ranch. He called it the Dead Cow Ranch. This was his brand:

He called it Tits up!

Twenty years later Billy Bob's luck is still holdin' true. He's gotta nice place and a fine young son he called Billy Bob Junior. Bubba is still draggin' along, toughin' it out and he has a beautiful daughter named Wava Dean.

Bubba came home late one evenin' on one of them cold, windy March days. Where the flag looks like it's ironed against the sky. He'd been workin' on a calvy heifer since noon; pulled the three point hitch off the tractor, broke three log chains and tore the frame outta the barn door. He sat down at the table in his usual despair. He reached around behind the gun case where he always kept a big jug of 'grape Nehi.' He's a suckin' on that jug when his darlin' wife come to the kitchen door.

"Bubber, honey, I gotta talk to ya 'bout something."
"Can't you see I'm wore out . . . Jus' let me set a minute . . ."
"Bubber, it's important. It's about our daugher, Wava Dan. You know, our daughter?"

50

"'Course I know'er! She's been livin' here nineteen years! You're probably gonna tell me she's in the 'family way'."

"Oh, Bubber, I'm sorry to say it, that's right!"

"Dadgummit! I mighta known! And I know who did it, too. Billy Bob's boy!"

He jumped outta the chair, run out and leaped in the pickup, threw gravel all over the front porch and peeled over to Billy Bob's ranch. 'Course the pickup broke down at the cattle guard and he had to walk all the way up the lane. Lost both five buckles. His luck was runnin' true.

Now, Billy Bob seen him comin' up the drive and met him at the door. "Come in, Bubba, I know all about it. I talked to my boy and I know why yer here. I'm gonna do all I can to make it right. Set down and have a drink." He poured him a big ol' shot of . . . grape Nehi.

"Now let me tellya what I'm gonna do. Tomorrow I'll take them kids down and buy'em a big diamond ring. We'll make the announcement and hav'em a big wedding. I'll pay fer it all. Then I'm gonna set up a hundred thousand dollar trust fund fer these kids."

All this time Bubba ain't sayin' nuthin.' Just settin' there drippin' all over the front of his shirt. Finally, Billy Bob says, "What's the matter with you, Bubba? These things happen and I'm doin' my best to make it right! Ain't you got nothin' to say?"

Bubba looked up at his ol' pardner and said, "Billy Bob, can we bring'er back if she ain't settled?"

LOUIE AND THE TONGS

Let me tell ya about Louie.

We's workin' a bunch of replacement heifers one year up on the Little Willow. Louie runs the cows. It wuz kind of a hot day an' we's workin' those critters through the chutes.

Clyde and Monte wuz there and they wuz pushin'em in. I wuz runnin' the squeeze and Louie wuz runnin' the head catch.

What Louie'd do is reach around an' grab the heifer as she come in and pull'er up snug so I could draw a little blood outta the jugular. It wuz sure hot! August. Louie'd reach down, pick up the nose tongs and slap 'em on. Then when we's done he'd jus' throw them tongs back on the ground and let'er out.

'Bout the middle of the second day it dawned on him that it was shore tiresome work bendin' over and pickin' up them tongs every time so he tied the shank of the nose tongs onto his belt. Tied 'em good! Then all he had to do when one come in wuz jus' grab that shank, flip'er up and catch them tongs and snap 'em on, dally and drag'er up! Then when he wuz done he'd jus' drop 'em an' he didn't have to bend over and pick 'em up every time.

Oh, he wuz proud! We got to braggin' on him. He got to flippin' it behind his back, through his legs and around his head. Kinda broke up the monotony of the day.

Then one of these heifers come a roarin' in! She stuck both her front feet through that Teco head catch along with her head! Louie got her mashed down good and I had her hip-locked with the squeeze. I hollered for Louie to get ahold of her head and I jumped over on the head bar and set on it while Louie run up and grabbed her.

Now, Louie's a big fella and he grabbed her around the neck like a bulldogger and held her there. He reached down with his left hand and snapped them tongs on her snout, and I'll be danged if she didn't git out!

Off we went! Just as she escaped I got her by the tail with both hands and in two jumps she wuz goin' flat out! I was sailin' behind her like a water skier! Louie wuz running neck an' neck with her 'round that corral tryin' to keep slack in the line, untie the knot and keep from gettin' drug to death!

He wuddn't havin' any luck.

He's tryin' to keep his eye peeled for the railroad ties and old posts layin' around the corral. She never even slowed down when she hit the trash barrel and set junk to flyin' everywhere!

Louie wuz runnin' right beside her, boy, takin' great big steps, his eyes were 'bout that big around and he kept screamin', "Don't let'er go boys, don't let'er go!"

She stopped in the corner and we all wuz heavin', tryin' to catch our breath and I wuz doubled over with laughter!

Out of the side of my vision, through my teary eyes, I seen a hand reach out an' flip that bar on the Powder River gate and that gate swung open real easy. The heifer spied the opening and shot through that hole like a rocket!

Boy! Straight out into the big corral makin' a bee-line for the pasture gate and about half way across'er I jus' couldn't tak'er any more and crashed to the ground. The dust is boilin' up and the last thing I see 'fore I go down is Louie out on the end of that tong rope, swingin' like a rock in David's slingshot!

When the dust settled he was layin' there up against the fence in a crumpled heap, fingering the broken end of the rope like the beads on his rosary.

ᘓ

THE LOST DOG

Evenin' Joe . . .
I hope I didn't wake y'all, I know it's after nine
But I got a little problem, so to speak.
I don't know how to tell this, I feel a little dumb
'Cause the little dog I had run off last week.

Yea, that bouncin' blue-eyed mongrel,
you know the one I mean.
He rides with me and sleeps on Mother's lap.
We got 'im when the kids left just a year or two ago
And I reckon that he sorta fills a gap.

I was up on Saddle Mountain to scatter out some salt
And he musta fell out when I started home.
I came out down by yer place and if he shows up there
I'd appreciate a jingle on the phone.

He really isn't worth much but Ma got plum upset.
Seems 'round the ranch he's made himself a star.
No, I'm not really worried, but the way she carried on
I better find him, ya know how women are.

I've phoned all of the neighbors and backtracked to the camp
And called for him until my throat is sore.
And I really wouldn't bother but I like the little cuss . . .
Just a minute, Joe, there's someone at the door.

Hello, Joe. You'll never guess! Ma, come take a look at this!
He's back! Say, Joe, I'll see you at the brandin'.
You crazy little buggar, come sit in Daddy's lap . . .
See ya, Joe. And Joe, thanks for understandin'.

CR

TINKER AND LADY

A stranger hanging' around cow workin's, sale barns or gatherin's
might get the impression that little love exists between the cowboy
and his dog. Only that the dog suffers from verbal abuse or that
the cowboy is entitled to sue for mental exasperation! Neither is
prone to open displays of affection. The cowboy acts tough and
the dog acts bored.

But I remember one time up at the Grouse Creek Ranch. It
was in the fall and we were workin' cows. Tinker was the
cook. It wasn't that he was a great cook but he'd always done
it and traditions get established regardless of their intrinsic
worth. He made a big pot of chili and beans the first night. It
was enough to feed the seven of us plus any visiting cavalry
platoon that might be billeting in the area! After supper we all
loaded in the pickup and drove fifteen miles to Pop's ranch.

Pop had a natural hot springs on his place. We bathed and soaked, loaded up and drove back to our ranch. On arrival Tinker realized we'd left his little dog, Lady, back at Pop's. Nobody really worried but Tinker backtracked anyway. The rest of us slept peacefully (the chili and beans was fresh.)

Next morning we stumbled into breakfast. The familiar aroma of chili and beans filled the kitchen. Unusual breakfast fare, but nobody said anything. Tinker looked like a dyin' duck in a thunderstorm! He'd been out all night lookin' for Lady.

Tinker was preoccupied all morning. He reheated the chili and beans for lunch. By supper (chili and beans) Tinker had become irritable. He'd walk to the window or outside every few minutes lookin' down the road and whistlin'. That night we slept with the doors and windows open in the bunkhouse.

At breakfast an unpleasant déjà vu lay heavy over the table. The chili and beans was the consistency of South Dakota gumbo and smelled like burning brakes. Tinker spoke to no one . . . all day. For supper we had chili and bean sludge. It was the closest I've come to eating lava. That night we slept outside.

Complaining to the cook is bad cowboy etiquette, but we all agreed something had to be done. Had a submarine trained its sonar on our stomachs he'd have thought he was picking up a pod of nauseous killer whales!

Breakfast the third day was fried adobe that tasted vaguely of chili and beans. We ate in silence accompanied by the growling sounds of indigestion and explosive borborygmi. Then we heard a scratching at the door. Tinker jumped up and looked! There was Lady, sore footed, dusty and glad to be home! Tinker picked her up like a baby and hugged her. She licked his face.

Still holding her, he took a big T-bone steak out of the frig and slapped it in the frying pan. After a couple turns he put it on the floor in front of her. She ate all she could and lay down, exhausted. Needless to say, we were happy for them both but we tried to act like it was no big deal so Tinker wouldn't be embarrassed. After he left, we dove for the bone!

IF HEREFORDS WERE BLACK

If Herefords were black and Angus were red
would breeders of Herefords breed Angus instead?
I mean, would the people who bred Herefords first
be now breeding Angus if things were reversed.

Or would they be loyal to red, white and true
To color of cowlick be always true blue?
If such were the case would they dis all the blacks,
Tell jokes about prolapse, compare them to Yaks

More suited for saddle or wearin' a yoke
Than stubbornly breeding until they go broke.
And those of the Aberdeen Angus cartel,
would they tout maternal endowments, as well,

Promoting their native resistence to thorns,
while cursing as mutants those not sprouting horns.
Just draggin' their sheath through the cheatgrass and burrs
like leaky ol' bass boats nobody insures.

Debate would rage on like it does anyway
if South had worn blue or the North had worn gray,
Or if Henry Ford had been Hank Chevrolet
You'd still be a Ford man... or would you, today?

So if Herefords were black and Angus were red
would breeders of Herefords breed Angus instead?
The question begs deep philosophical thought
but don't get disgruntled or get overwrought

The breeders of purebreds run true to the grain
And efforts to change them would just be in vain
And not 'cause they think other cattle are bad
"I'm stickin' with this one, 'cause that's what Dad had."

Illustration: Charlie Marsh

57

ONE MORE YEAR

Every fall when I go out to preg check the cows I find a few that,
so far as I'm concerned, need cullin'. So I point out the reasons
in my best professional manner and cut her off to the side but
that don't always seem to satisfy the cowboy runnin' the cows.
Now they wouldn't ever admit to likin' one of them ol' shells but
they recall her better days and want'a make sure she's had every
chance. So the conversation between the green young vet'inary
and the experienced rancher goes somethin' like this . . .

WHAT'S THE STORY ON THAT GOOD OL' COW?
The bow-legged cowboy asked.
>   She's sorta gimpy on the left hind leg
>   And her breathin's kinda fast.

SHUCKS! I REMEMBER WHEN SHE WUZ BORNED
IT WUDDN'T THAT LONG AGO.
>   Well, somebody bobbed her tail last year
>   But, shoot, I guess you oughta know.

YOU BET YER LIFE! I KNOW THAT COW!
SHE'S AS GOOD A ONE AS I'VE SAW!
>   I jus' thought since she's getting thin
>   And gotta big lump on her jaw.

THAT AIN'T NOTHIN'! JUST A LITTLE KNOT!
The bow-legged cowboy said.
>   Yeah, but one eye's blue and she leppied her calf
>   And she ain't gotta tooth in her head.

LISTEN KID, I 'MEMBER THAT COW!
WHY, I EVEN MILKED'ER FER A WHILE!
>   Sure but she's gotta swing bag an' one big tit
>   And skin like a crocodile!

KID! YOU GOTTA ADMIT SHE KNOWS THE RANGE
AND EVERY WATER HOLE!
>   I hate to tell ya she's open now
>   And these prolapse stitches won't hold.

SHE'S NOTHIN' TO ME, DON'T GIT ME WRONG,
I KNOW SHE'S GETTIN' OLD,
>   Well, yer the boss, if you want'a keep her
>   Whatever you say goes

>   But if it'uz me I'd cull'er fast
>   And never shed a tear.
WELL...I GOTTA LITTLE GRASS OUT BEHIND THE HOUSE...
LET'S RUN HER ANOTHER YEAR.

Illustration: Don Gill

59

GRAFTIN' CALVES

"I was ugly when I was born." "How ugly were you?" "I was so ugly they had to tie my mother's legs together so I could nurse!" If you've ever grafted a calf you know just what I'm talkin' about.

In the old days when a cowman had a heifer that had lost her calf, he'd kick her out and let her heal up. He'd run her with the bull that spring and give her a second chance. Then...he sent his kid to ag school! She returned full of knowledge and explained to him that runnin' a cow without a calf is not a sound economic practice. The solution was to graft an orphan calf onto the heifer.

Not as easy as the Extension pamphlet might indicate! That heifer has learned through eons of evolutional instinct not to take something that is not hers. But, we're going to trick her!

Picture this heifer, she has just gone through the most traumatic period in her young life. She's exhausted, she weighs 750 lbs, her tailhead sticks up like a shark's fin and she's got a bag the size of a teacup! You go to town and come back with a 150 pound Holstein bull calf!

Ever since the time of Noah's Livestock Auction and Commission Company, peddlers have been offering magical formulae that guarantee the heifer will take the calf! Every cowman I know has a secret formula that worked for him once twenty years ago. He wants *you* to try it. Different scents abound: musk from a rutting beaver, compost drops, eucalyptus oil, Limburger lotion or grizzly after shave. They all have one thing in common, they smell like two dead carp in a Hefty trash bag on a warm Phoenix afternoon!

I've tried 'em all. I even used the ol' sheepherder's trick of skinnin' the dead calf and putting the hide on a live calf. A procedure that takes both of 'em off the best dressed list in the wink of an eye!

My most effective method uses a very subtle technique. One so delicate and difficult to describe, that it may be truly understood only by the most devout attender of horse training clinics. It is cow psychology at its finest. I call it . . . SHOVEL TRAINING!

You put the heifer and orphan calf in a small pen and hobble the heifer. The calf goes to suck, she kicks at him. You hit her with the shovel! A firm tap on the poll is preferred.

Soon all you have to do is stand outside the pen and display the shovel. The heifer freezes in place! Eventually the calf gets the idea. He recognizes the sound of your pickup comin' down to the calvin' barn. You start down the alley. He's got his head through the gate wavin' you on. "Down here! Bring the shovel!"

I don't know if this method works on mules, kangaroos or Congressional aides, but I'd recommend it for yer good ol' run of the mill black bally.

CR

BULL FIGHT

The sound of train cars coupling rumbled through the frozen air
And struck a nerve in some primeval core.
Our horses started dancin', somethin' made their nostrils flare.
A premonition washed upon their shore.

We pushed 'em toward the clearing as their apprehension grew.
They snorted and began to steer like boats,
Prancing sideways, rollers blowing, hoofbeats pounding a tattoo,
Then a bellow! Our hearts jumped in our throats.

"They're at it," said young Cody as the bulls came into view.
His voice squeaked. Bulls can have that effect.
He glanced around half lookin' for a demolition crew
The way the lower meadow had been wrecked.

"Take it easy, lad," I told him, "They'll be lookin' for a fight.
I've seen 'em lift a horse clean off the ground.
Stick a horn right through their belly . . .
It'll make your hair turn white,
A skewered horse can make a hellish sound."

61

Then two bulls as big as boulders banged together head to head.
It sounded like the closing of a vault.
Tectonic plates colliding, their reverberation spread
Like tremors from the San Andreas fault.

They pushed with heads like anvils, bone as thick as two by fours
And circled, each one looking for a chance.
The ground beneath them pulverized, like waltzing dinosaurs,
Triceratops reborn for one last dance.

It dang sure wasn't pretty, see, one had a broken nose.
The blood was splattered up and down their sides.
It smelled like when you gut a buck and get it on your clothes,
A steaming green and red smeared on their hides.

The young bull slid a horn beneath the other's naked flank
And hooked him like an ax man felling trees.
The old one groaned and faltered,
the young one turned the crank
And drove the aged warrior to his knees.

"Looks like curtains for the geezer," Cody said with no regard
For differences existing in our age.
"It's the way of things," he told me. "The passin' of the guard.
The old must step aside and clear the stage."

One last lunge to finish off the ruler now dethroned.
It smashed into the beefy upturned hip.
But the peckin' order's fickle, no one savvy's the unknown . . .
The grass was slick, the young bull made a slip

And went down, his shoulder crunching. For a moment he lay still.
The old bull rose, no longer in defeat.
His shadow fell across his foe but never moved to kill.
The young bull stumbled quickly to his feet.

Horn to horn they eyed each other.
Then the old bull turned away.
Cody spoke, "I knew he'd finally get him."
"You underestimate," I said, "The depth of nature's sway.
If you ask me, I'd say the old bull let him."

62

Illustration: Dave Holl

JOSÉ AND THE HOODOO COW

We run this ol' cow in the squeeze chute,
she rattled and fought all the way
Then rammed a hind foot through the side bars
and managed to cow-kick José.

He dropped the syringe he was holdin'.
It stuck in the toe of his boot,
'Least, now he's protected from Lepto.
He gave her the gringo salute!

She wedged a big horn in the head gate
and dang near flipped onto her side.
It occurred to me, not for the first time
how nicer she'd be . . . chicken fried.

She thrashed and created a shambles
of everything not battened down.
She moved the whole chute off its footing
and knocked poor José to the ground.

We finally, somehow, got her captured
and squeezed with her head stickin' out.
My job was to check on her dentures.
I carefully reached for the snout.

She buried her nose to the hubcaps
and watched with her little pig eye
'Til my body leaned into the strike zone
then she swung her head like a scythe!

"She's old!" I yelled, as she grazed my ribs.
"Heck, you never looked," said the boss.
"Well, check'er yerself!" I shot back right quick,
"It could be my eyeballs were crossed!"

The vet plunged himself to the armpit,
in search of a pregnancy there.
I prayed every year she'd be open.
If God would just answer my prayer.

"She's bred!" Came the cry from the backside.
Like always I drew the short straw.

It looked like another long winter
with Darth Vader's mother-in-law.

José and I watched her departing.
We'd spent quite awhile with this bunch
And knew that ol' cow for a hoodoo
that dang sure would eat a man's lunch.

She'd climb up yer rope like a viper
and make a man hunt a new job
And any poor fool that dismounted
could wind up on her shish-kabob.

She might grab the lead when yer trailin'
or maybe just brush up and hide
But she'd take a horse in the willers
so you'd best be ready to ride.

I reminded José how we'd saved her
that time she got stuck in the bog.
I lost a good rope in the process,
she wallered José like a hog!

"You nearly got drownded, Amigo."
"Verdad. Muy mala, that cow.
If we'd have leaved her for the lobos,
my foot, she would not hurting now."

The boss was surveyin' the wreckage,
"I think this here tailgate is broke.
Say, José, did she git all her shots?"
José eyed the boss then he spoke,

"She's missing the one she's most needing.
La puerca's too much with her tricks."
"You mean," asked the boss, "Vitamin A?"
"Oh, no, Señor, thirty-ought-six!"

THE ROOSTER WITH SPURS

Down at the Smith Barn one day we wuz calvin' first calf heifers. Now a lot of the boys that don't speak English real good have to make up their own names for the gringos. They have trouble sayin' them English names like Carruthers or Mackintosh and the like. They sound common to us but they ain't common to them. Their name for Dale is, "El Gallo con Espuelas" which is "the Rooster with Spurs." He does kinda walk with his chest out, sorta cocky and wears them big ol' jinglin' rowels. Always wears a bright scarf.

He come a'stridin' in down there one mornin' pretty early just dressed up fit to kill. Brand new shirt and everything! Really proud! George had been there all night and he had a heifer in the squeeze chute tryin' to pull this calf. He'd pulled fer all he's worth and wuz plum give out. Dale saw him and said, "Whattsa matter? Can't you pull that calf? Git outta the way and let me do it!"

George wuddn't 'bout to argue. He'd been workin' on him fer a while anyway.

Dale stepped around there behind the heifer, propped his feet up against the bottom of the chute, grabbed a'holt of them two OB handles and jis' rared back!

The calf wuz comin' straight out and had his head jus' right, he's a big calf wuz all. Dale, whenever he gits to doin' somethin' he grits his teeth and smiles jus' like a jack-o-lantern and squints his eyes. He had a good grip and wuz leaned back like a water skier.

As the calf started to come, that nice smooth little round forehead on the calf pressed up on the heifer's rectum and cleaned it slicker'n a whistle! There was a stream 'bout an eighth of an inch thick and two inches wide came arcin' out like a rainbow. It jus' missed the brim of Dale's hat an' splattered all over his face, in his mouth and down the front of his shirt. He couldn't do nothin' cause he was rared back so far. If he'da let go he'da fell flat on his back! So he jus' hung on 'til the calf came out and crashed in a soggy pile on top of him!

We went over and dragged the calf offa him. Dale came to life spittin' and cussin'! He raised his head just in time to see that heifer, pretty as ya please, clean the afterbirth right in his lap!

TAXIDERMY HEIFER

As the only local cow vet, Steve had calved a lot of heifers
And as such was most reluctant to keep score
'Cause no matter how he tried and tried, he couldn't save them all
So on the side he opened up a taxidermy store.

"Stuff yer heifer," was his motto, it was on his business cards.
And the message he recorded on the phone
Said, "If I can't save her, you can! As a conversation piece.
Have her mounted or just standing there alone."

He stuffed them in positions that he thought might catch the eye
One leg upraised her milking on a tire
Or rearing up like Trigger, or with X's on her eyes
Surrounded by a priest and candles waiting to expire.

There were action poses in the stance of how she last appeared
Like on her back, a huge midline incision
Or standing with the calf half out, feet first, the hind legs showing
That looked like some real bad rear end collision!

Or head down in the charging mode, about to mow you down,
The water bag a timeless counterweight.
Or half a mount, just the backside, with his OB chains protruding
As he last saw her going out the gate.

The market for his HEIFERS-IN-DISTRESS grew leaps and bounds,
His cuddly cows kept flying out the doors.
People put them on the mantle, people placed them on the lawn
Like pink flamingos grazing on all fours.

Until, alas, some thought they saw conflict going on
'tween his practice and his taxidermy shop.
"These charges pain me deeply," he told his vet technician,
"My reputations's always been the top.

"What makes them think I'd compromise my veterinary work
To make a little money on the side?"
"Well, they might be misinterpreting
your heifer calving price," she said.
"Not many charge a hundred dollars . . . and the hide."

SELLIN' PREWITT'S COW

Now these ol' boys that own sale barns have occasion to speculate on an ol' cow now and then. They buy her, feed her a week or two, then try and slip'er back through the sale. They get down in the ring to keep her good side to the crowd. They look up at the auctioneer, and he begins:

Hey, bid alright, sir . . . step right up
we're gonna sell this fine cow.

I've got a 5 dollar bid on a cow,
a good cow, who'll bid ten . . .
Walkin' on three, milkin' on two . . .
You ain't got ten, I ain't through.

"Cause I'll take eight, give the eight . . .
This cow's great . . .
One big foot and one bad ear
What do you care if she can't hear!

Nothin's wrong you can't fix . . .
You won't give eight, I'll take six!
Six big bills. C'mon try . . .
She don't need but one good eye.

What do you mean she ain't alive!
See her breathin' . . . I'll take five.
C'mon boys, you make me sore . . .
CALL THE VET . . . I'll take four!

Four ain't much, she's just a pup . . .
C'MON PREWITT, GIT'ER UP!
C'mon boys, nothin's free . . .
GIT THE TRACTOR . . . I'll take three!

Three is all I'm askin' now . . .
Surely someone needs this cow!
You may think that I'm all through . . .
There's still a chance . . . I'll take two!

68

PREWITT, GIT'ER PROPPED UP STRAIGHT . . .
LEAN'ER UP AGAINST THE GATE!
Fine replacement, bled and pregged . . .
Pay no mind to that bad leg.

She's a dandy, not too old . . .
Tits'll grow back so I'm told . . .
Rigor mortis? . . . No just tense . . .
Someone give me 50 cents!

Anybody give a dime?
Hurry up! There ain't much time!
C'mon boys . . . use your head . . .
DANG IT PREWITT, NOW SHE'S DEAD!

NIGHT MAN IN THE HEIFER LOT

I came on just after supper. Boss had fixed a little sheep camp
with a bed and propane burner so a feller could have coffee in
the middle of the night.

On my first check it was quiet in my bunch of calvy heifers and
the moonlight made the cedars look like postcards,
I was thinkin' all was good and all was right.

But at ten I found two mamas with their water bags a'showin'.
They were off there in a corner so I left'em to their business
and went back to fill my mug.

In an hour one showed progress. Heifers take a little longer,
but the other needed checkin' so I worked her to the calvin' barn
and put her in a jug.

Pullin' calves is always chancy like yer playin' slots in Vegas,
Put yer hand in - pull the lever - double front feet or the head
back, nothin' comin' but the tail.

But tonight my luck was runnin',
head and feet were pointin' at me
so I chained 'em up and gently helped him make a change of
address. Like deliverin' the mail.

I administered a rub down, swung him upside down a second,
stuck a straw up to his nostril, watched him fill his lungs
un-aided with his first taste of fresh air.

Then I loosed the heifer's halter.
She was quick to start his lessons.
Soon her baby found the fountain, tail a'ringin', he was suckin'
in his calfskin underwear.

By coincidence I noticed back behind in yonder corner
that the other heifer also had her baby up and suckin'
and was puttin' on a show.

It was sorta satisfyin'. I admit I paused a minute
to appreciate life's mysteries, although mostly I was thinkin'
only ninety-six to go.

Illustration: Charlie Marsh

THE CALVING NIGHTY

I slept and dreamed of sunny beaches,
sea shells, sand and kelp.
"I'VE GOT HER IN THE CALVING BARN.
I'M GONNA NEED SOME HELP."
The waves were crashing over me,
the sea gulls dived and ducked.
"SHE CALVED ALL RIGHT ALL BY HERSELF
BUT JUNIOR'S NEVER SUCKED."

I woke to find my husband up and lookin' woebegone.
"IT'LL ONLY TAKE A MINUTE,
YOU CAN LEAVE YOUR NIGHTY ON."
Next thing I know I'm in the barn. It smelled like creosote.
I'd pulled on his old overshoes and my ol' chorin' coat.

"IF YOU'LL DISTRACT THE COW,"
he said, a little bleary eyed,
"I'LL TRY AND GATHER UP THE CALF
WHILE SHE'S PREOCCUPIED."
I tried to make a feeble wave. She didn't take the bait.
"YOU'VE GOT TO JUMP AROUND A BIT.
JUST CLIMB UP ON THE GATE."

I stepped up on the second board
and yelled with all my might.
She nearly did a somersault! I caught her eye alright.
She charged the panel where I stood, I felt the crackin' pine.
I leaped and grabbed a rafter like ol' Tarzan would a vine.

The overshoes flew off my feet, I wrapped my legs around
And hung there like a three toed sloth, my nighty hangin' down.
The cow was blowin' slobbers on my winter lingerie.
It soon became a sodden mess, exposed my exposé.

I tried to save some dignity but it was fading fast.
I felt like a piñata with a bullseye on my . . . person.
Each charge she'd hook my nighty and make a bigger rip
Until I felt her cuddy breath condensing on my hip.

I'm screamin' for my hubby when he finally reappeared.
The panel lay in splinters and the cow had disappeared.
"What took so long!" I shouted as I dangled overhead.
The tears were streaming down his face,
he caught his breath and said,

"I DUMPED THE CALF AND BANGED MY HEAD
AND TRIED TO RACE RIGHT BACK
WHEN A MOMENTARY VISION UP
AND STOPPED ME IN MY TRACK.
A NURSERY RHYME ABOUT A DISH
THAT RAN AWAY WITH A SPOON
AND THERE BEFORE MY VERY EYES
THE COW JUMPED OVER THE MOON!"

It was a sorry explanation but at least I thought he tried.
I couldn't keep a straight face.
We both laughed until we cried.
He still talks about my bravery and the time I used my clout
And showed'em what Victoria's big secret's all about!

∞

PROLAPSE FROM THE BLACK LAGOON

It came from outta nowhere, like a prolapse in the night.
Which, in fact is what it was, my friends,
the cow vet's scourge and plight.
That pudgy pink projectile from those monster movie scenes
Like some whopping giant burrito filled with attitude and beans.

I was soon laid down behind it on a hillside in the muck
While the cowboy shined his high beams
from his perch there in the truck.
His rope stretched from the bumper
to her front legs tied in haste.
As I wallowed in the darkness like a frog, stripped to the waist.

It was bigger than a tree trunk. It was slick as old chow mein.
It was heavy as a carpet someone left out in the rain.
I tried to gain some purchase as I pressed my fist in tight,
It was like a thrashing porpoise and was putting up a fight.

I got it in a hammerlock. It was like a rabid dog.
I wrapped my legs around it like a monkey on a log.
I pushed until my shoulder disappeared inside the mass
As I scrabbled for a foothold in the mud and frozen grass.

73

But alas, with one huge effort she expelled me from her grip.
I shot out like a cannon, rolled and did a double flip
But I grabbed her tail in passing
and with strength born out of war,
I dove at the appendage like some punch drunk matador.

I lifted her hind quarters, and I swung her side to side,
Then, like smart men do, I used my head to push it back inside!
It was dark there for a second, it was hard to catch my breath
But there she lay, my patient I had saved from certain death.

The cowboy rolled his window down, said,
"Doc, are you alright?"
He gunned the engine several times.
The headlights got real bright.
"I've seen a prolapse done before but never quite like that!"
"Oh, they taught us that in vet school . . .
But I think it ate my hat."

∞

COW ATTACK

"What happened to your pickup seat? Is that buffalo track?"
Well, I guess you had to be there. We had a cow attack.
It all began when me and Roy went out to check the cows.
We'd finished lunch, watched RFD
and forced ourselves to rouse.

We's pokin' through the heavy bunch for calves to tag and check.
I spotted one but his ol' mom was bowin' up her neck.
She pawed the ground and swung her head
a'slingin' froth and spit
Then bellered like a wounded bull.
"Say, Roy," I said, "let's quit!"

But Roy was bent on taggin' him and thought to make a grab.
"Just drive up there beside the calf, I'll pull him in the cab."
Oh, great. Another stroke of genius, of cowboy derring do.
Surnuf when Roy nabbed the calf, his mama came in too.

And I do mean climbed up in there! Got a foot behind the seat,
Punched a horn right through the windshield
and she wasn't very neat.

She was blowin' stuff out both ends til the cab was slick and green.
It was on the floor and on the roof and on the calf vaccine.

If you've been inside a dryer at the local laundromat
With a bear and fifty horseshoes then you know just where I's at.
At one point she was sittin' up, just goin' for a ride
But then she tore the gun rack down, the calf jumped out my side.

I was fightin' with my door lock
which she'd smashed a'passin' by
When she peeked up through the steering wheel
and looked me in the eye.
We escaped like paratroopers out the window, landed clear
But the cow just kept on drivin' 'cause the truck was still in gear.

She topped a hump and disappeared. The blinker light came on
But if she turned I just can't say, by then the truck was gone.
I looked at Roy, "My truck's a wreck.
My coveralls are soaked.
I'll probably never hear again. I think my ankle's broke.

And look at you. Yer pitiful. All crumbled up and stiff.
Like you been eat by wild dogs and pooped over a cliff."
"But think about it," Roy said, "Since Grandpa was alive,
I b'lieve that that's the firstest time I've seen a cattle drive."

Illustration: Don Gill

75

THE ROMANTIC COWBOY

There's nothing like an evening of calving to promote the romantic image of the cowboy. Right, ladies?

Don invited a nice woman out to his ranch one evening for candlelight, wine and canned bean dip. This dinner date coincided with calving season. After an hour of civilized conversation about French paintings, the European Common Market and the condition of the rodeo arena in Ponoka, Don invited his date to go with him to check the cows.

She didn't exactly squeal with delight but he explained how scientific livestock raising had become. "Almost like visiting a human hospital maternity ward," he said, authoritatively.

They drove his Bronco out into the calving pasture and immediately spotted a braymer cross cow tryin' to calve. "We'll watch her for a few minutes to see if everything comes out okay," suggested Don sliding an arm around her shoulders.

They sat in the warm cab, moonlight mixing with Don's elaborate discourse of bovine parturition. After half an hour he decided to assist the cow. Partly for the cow and partly to show off.

The calf appeared to be hiplocked.

His date prepared to see modern veterinary procedure save the day. Don drove up to the head end of the cow and left the headlights shining in her eyes. Sneaking out, he slipped around behind her. He slid the nylon obstetrical straps over the calf's protruding front feet. At first tug the cow arose like a bee stung buffalo!

She whirled to mash Don. He was jerked off his feet but clung to the straps as the cow chased him like a dog chasin' its tail! He was alternately upright, flat out, levitating, scooting, skiing, sliding, screaming and squirreling as the three of them circled like a shaky ceiling fan.

His only hope of survival was to hang on and stay behind the helicoptering cow. Even then she managed to land enough blows to win the round and tromp his fallen hat to a pulp.

On one mighty jerk, the calf popped out. Don executed a complete cartwheel and landed on his back. The cow rolled him once and headed off in the darkness.

His date, who had watched Don's calving technique from the cab was not impressed. "Less than professional," she had commented as he climbed in the cab after giving the departed cow a four alarm cussing.

Don tried to regain his composure and recapture the mood by explaining that he had been in control the whole time. However, it was not very convincing what with the big glob of manure plastered on the side of his neck and the piece of placenta dangling from his ear.

❧

WANDA AND THE WILD HEIFER

It was a cold starry night somewhere in West River, Dakotaland. Calving had been under way a couple weeks. Ed and Wanda were already into the heifer checking routine.

On this particular night Wanda had taken the middle-of-the-night duty. Ed had stayed up late trying to fix a water leak in the barn. Water pipes are buried deep up north. Ed had dug a hole big enough to bury a small mulc. Grunt work – frozen ground, mud under the permafrost. He located the break, shut off the main line and called it quits for the night.

After Wanda reheated supper for him, he hit the hay. It was midnight and he fell asleep, exhausted. Wanda set her alarm for 2:30 am. She'd make the deep in the night heifer check and let Ed rest. Ranch wives are the unsung work force in the glamorous panorama of the romantic life of the cowboy.

Imagine, if you will, instead of billboards depicting the handsome, macho Marlboro Man, you see a full color spread of a red-faced woman with steamed up glasses wearing lumpy, well-used canvas coveralls, her nighty wadded up around her waist, poking out above the zipper, maybe a torn down jacket with dehorning blood on the sleeve, hair sticking out underneath a ratty wool stocking cap, mismatching gloves and muddy slip-on rubberized moon boots that look more like deer liver than clothing.

The alarm woke Wanda. She bundled up and stomped out to the barn. She moved one nervous heifer from the calving lot into the barn. The heifer did not like the move and got on the fight. Wanda tried to bluff. It didn't work. The heifer charged! Wanda scrambled over the portable panels that comprised the sides of the pen and fell...right into the hole Ed had dug earlier. The heifer tried to jump the panels after her but succeeded only in knocking it over – right on top of the hole, trapping Wanda underneath.

Then, just when you were thinking, 'poor Wanda,' the heifer landed feet first on top of the panel, driving all four legs down through the bars.

Wanda lay flat on her back as four bovine cloven hooves paddled furiously 12 inches above her frayed and frigid evening wear. It was like the fish-eye view of swimming cows.

Four hours later Ed woke up, shaved, made the coffee, and came out to the barn looking for the love of his life.

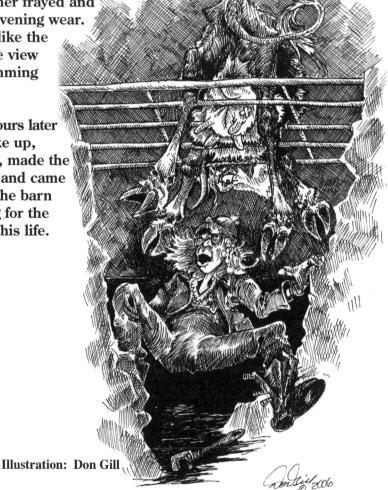

Illustration: Don Gill

GERALD TWO BEARS AND BILLY STRIKE

Gerald Two Bears was the foreman of the tribal branding crew.
Lots of Indians who were cowboys came to do what they could do.
Billy Strike was good at roping and his medicine was strong
And he roped 'em automatic 'til misfortune come along!

He roped a good-sized heifer calf, but he roped her 'round the neck.
She ran behind his horse's butt and put 'em both in check!
The rope slid underneath his tail which spooked the pony some,
So, of course, he went to pitchin'! 'Cause the nylon chafed his bum!

Now like I said, that Billy's tough and wouldn't quit his dally,
The rope was holdin' him down tight! Made every peak and valley!
His horse was snorting up the dirt like he was sweepin' mines
And kickin' himself sideways like a spring when it unwinds!

Billy blew his left hand stirrup, so he leaned against the tide
But his saddle got some cockeyed, slippin' off the other side.
His dally peeled off the horn! His anchor chain had broke!
Billy flew like Humpty Dumpty and came down
and broke his yolk!

Gerald Two Bears ran to Billy, who lay still upon the ground.
He said, "Billy, are you alright?" Billy never made a sound.
He listened for his breathing but he lay so awfully still
He said, *"Billy, can you hear me?"* Then with superhuman will

Billy's eyelid raised, the eyeball
turned and swiveled toward the source,
Gerald leaned up close and whispered,
"Billy, can I have your horse?"

79

FEAR OF FLYING

Andy summed up flying the best I've heard: "If yer gonna have to land in a field, always land *with* the rows!"

Although I had a momentary lapse of good judgement once and took a week's worth of flying lessons, I have since left that task up to more serious folks; People who don't stay up all night celebrating and can actually reset the hands on a digital watch!

I know cowboys that are pilots. It's a frightening combination, akin to a CPA who does nude modeling on the side! All they talk about is flying and if there's two at your table, your brain goes numb after five minutes! It's like being trapped in a pickup on the road from Broadus to Billings between two cuttin' horse people!

But for good reason many western ranchers have taken up flying. They can check windmills, count cows and chase coyotes without having to open a gate. Roy hired a local boy out of Chadron to pilot him over his ranch to thin out the coyote population. The plane was a single engine Super Cub. The side door is dropped and the hunter straps himself in and leans out the door, cannon in hand. It is not a job for the fainthearted.

The pilot followed Roy's directions and was soon swooping down on the crafty coyotes while Roy blazed away with his twelve gauge. Suddenly the plane began to shake like a wet dog! The vibration loosened Roy's upper plate and the pilot's *I'd Rather Be Flying* T-shirt began to unravel! Roy, in his near-sighted exuberance, had led the coyote too much and shot the tip off the one propeller blade!

With heroic control, the young pilot landed the plane on an old stretch of rutted wagon road. He shut 'er down and staggered out into the sagebrush, visibly shaken.

He didn't care that he was twenty miles from the ranch headquarters and facin' a long walk back in the company of a crusty old rancher who had spit all over the side of his plane. He was just thankful to be on the ground!

His prayers were interrupted by an explosion! He dived for the dirt and smashed his new aviator sunglasses in the process! He looked back and Roy was standing in front of the plane holding the smoking twelve gauge.

"I evened 'em up, Sonny. She ought to fly okay now." He'd shot the tip off the other end of the prop!

Did they make it home? You bet yer shirt tail they did! It vibrated a little bit, but no worse than drivin' down a railroad track at a 120 mph!

CR

LOST

A source of pride amongst cowboys
Is knowin' the lay of the land
And any poor fool that gets lost
They figger ain't much of a hand!

They said, "We'll meet up at Bull Crick!"
Then looked at me like a trainee!
*"Draw me a map and I'll find it!
Columbus had nothin' on me!"*

Daylight broke into my windshield,
Headed south and loaded for bear.
I turned at the Grasmere station
I should'a shot myself right there!

Nothin' was like they described it,
No mailbox where it should be,
No coyote hide on the fence post,
Now where's Mary's Crick s'posed to be?

Their map showed tourist attractions
Including, I swear, Noah's Ark!
Little ol' tricklin' Sheep Creek
Was wider than Yellowstone Park!

I crossed the Cow and the Horse Crick
And cricks named for Nickles and Dimes
Through Nit Crick, Louse Crick and Crab Crick,
Crossed Willer Crick twenty-eight times!

Driving demented and crazy!
A'chasin' my tail like a dog!
Coursing through desert and mountain,
Brush thicket and cattail bog!

Fighting back panic, I'm thinkin',
'I could die and never be found!
Worse yet, I'll look like a gunsel
Who can't find his way outta town!'

Harold was the boss of the truckers.
I figgered he might set me right.
So, I called him up on the two-way
And explained my desperate plight.

He said, "Describe yer surroundings."
I looked for a landmark somewhere.
"Ain't nothin' but rocks and sagebrush!"
He said, *"Sonny, yer almost there!"*

Illustration: Charlie Marsh

WAITING FOR DADDY

"Mama, when's Daddy comin' home? Is it time to worry yet?"
"By supper, darlin'. Eat your Cheerios."
He rode out this morning early. Like he does six days a week
I always make him tell me where he goes
'Specially when I know he's headed over on the canyon side
At least I know I'll have a place to start
So in case he doesn't come back I can hunt for him myself
Or go for help if I get faint of heart

"Run and git your schoolbooks, kiddos! And be sure to
    wash yer hands." "Aw Mama, do we have to school today?"
If it wasn't for homeschooling I might lose what mind I've got
It helps to pass the daylight time away
And I know I shouldn't worry but I worry anyway
Who wouldn't, if they were in my shoes
I've been up those rocky canyons and I've seen those snaky trails
I know how quick a horse can blow a fuse

"Mama, Cody said a swear word." "I did not!" "Did too!"
"Did not! I only said Ring went to the commode."
Oh, thank God I've got these children just to keep me occupied
But still I'm always lookin' down the road
All afternoon I've watched the sky. It's like I'm playin' poker
You don't know how I fear an angry cloud
And the wind gives me the shivers.
Never lets me drop my guard.
Nothin' like it whispers quite so loud

"Mama, when's Daddy comin' home? Shouldn't he be
    home by now? We wanna ride before it gets too dark."
And the hardest time for me I guess is now till six o'clock
I'm nervous till I hear the home dogs bark
But the kids are my salvation. 'Course, they wanna be like Dad
He saddles up their horse and lets'em go
And I stand here by the window thinkin' 'here we go again'
But they're cowboyin', the only life they know

"Mama, look! Oh, here comes Daddy. That's him trottin'
    up the road. He's wavin', now he's comin' through the gate."
"See, I told you kids be patient, not to get your dander up . . ."
And learn to wait, and wait and wait and wait.

THE DAY THE RANCH CHANGED HANDS

I first met the crew in the bunkhouse
the day that we bought the 4 D's.
I'd come in that night after supper
and found 'em all takin' their ease.

My job was to count all the cattle
and stay till the transfer was done.
I offered my hand to the cowboys
and asked how the outfit was run.

"My names ees Man'well Palomino. Vaquero. I came here to ride. The boss said ef I wass illegal, I only could work the outside. He put me down there on the desert, at Cow Creek. Eet wassn't a crime. They brought us the grocery on Tuesday an' that wass how we tol' the time. Four hunnred cows. Yus me an' a kid whose name I remember was Yak. Eet wass col'. I wass from Chihuahua but no way wass I goin' back. Jew remember Yak, doan jew, Tombstone? Jew wass here back then, ees por sure."

"Yeah. I's here when you hit the country. You was green as a pile of manure. You couldn't say nuthin' in English. Pore Jack, he'd forgot how to speak. When you guys come in for the brandin' he wouldn't shut up for a week! I wonder where Jack ever wound up. He didn't stay long around here. All I know's that spring I'd been workin' the 4 D's for over a year."

"Shoot, Tombstone, that must be a record! The boss says and swears that it's true that you worked more times for the outfit than anyone else he knew!"

"You stuff it, Mick! You burnt out ol' wreck. You spend half yer life underground. Catlow Rim's been dug up so much it looks like a prairie dog town. All winter you live in that line shack, prospectin' and minin' for gold. But . . . sure be nice if you hit a vein before we all git too dang old."

"Say, Mister, my name is Phil Duckett. I guess I'm the new buckaroo. You reckon the new 4 D owners will keep the same guys on the crew? When some of these ranches change owners they come in and clean out the place. It ain't no big deal if they do it, it's just that it seems such a waste. Like Manyul, he knows every canyon and Tombstone he knows every cow. Them hay meadows needs to be watered and Mick, he's the man that knows how. Even Pete, back there in the corner don't say much and always looks grim.

But he's a mechanical genius and nuthin' don't run without him.
Besides, he's been courtin' ol' Hazel, the cook that you'll meet in
the morn. Aw, now Pete, don't look at me that way. You know
I'm jus' honkin' yer horn. Joe Ben's livin' down in the small
house. He's young but a real top hand and his wife's expectin'
this summer. Her home grown tomatoes are grand."

"Perdon, Señor. Doan worry 'bout us. But I hope they keep
Meester Yim. I tink he's here for twenny-five years. A shame
eef they no hirin' him. Thees ranch he knows like the ears of
hiss horse. The trail's cut into hiss grain. He can draw any
creek or campo from a map on the back of hiss brain."

"Yup, he's a good boss and we know it to put up with misfits
like us. They can pick on me about Hazel but Jim is a man
you can trust. But let me just point out a factor. The nearest
town's sixty-five miles. Not too many men like the lonesome
and lonesome don't fit women's styles. The drifters we get, you
should see'em, that come in here lookin' for work. Most all
of'em runnin' from somethin', afflicted with some kinda quirk.
We even get hippies and outlaws. 'Course, buckaroos, they
come and go. But, a few of us, we're sorta home here and we
just thought someone should know. So keep us in mind when
you go back and if they ask how we might do, could you tell'em
. . . we fit the country an' put in a word for the crew."

I told'em I'd sure think it over.
We shook and I bid'em goodnight.
My bed was laid out at the main house
so I walked up there toward the light.

I paused in the cottonwood shadows
the moonlight had made in the lane
And soaked up the smell of the
sagebrush and the ozone promise of rain.

I could hear the murmur of voices
from the bunkhouse there for a spell.
No doubt they were hashin' things
over to see if they'd made their case well.

But men like these cowboys, I'd vouch for.
Was easy to cut'em some slack
'Cause twenty-one years this last winter,
Manuel had been callin' me Yak.

BLAZING BLOATS

"My Gosh! How'd you set yer hat on fire?
Snorting gunpower again?"
"Well, I didn't do it on purpose," he said,
Rubbing the spot on his chin.

Hie eyebrows were singed off uneven
And unsymmetrically skewed
While the glass was gone from his glasses
Which rendered him spectaclely nude.

"It was dark," he said, "You know methane will burn?
Me and Jake were out checkin' the stock.
We were comin' in late and found one
That looked like she needed the doc.

But we were both cow paramedics
Trained to do more than just ride
And savvied her dire situation
All bloated and laid on her side.

Not having a bloat hose or trocar,
First choices for saving her life,
I blindly palpated the left flank
For the place where I'd plunge in my knife.

I inserted the tip of my dagger,
It fit like a key in a latch
When Jake said, "Here let me help you!"
With a flourish the fool struck a match.

A blue flame roared out of the orifice
Like St. Helens come back from the dead!
A whoosh, like an airbag exploding
Pinned my ears back to my head!

I thought I'd been struck by lightning,
St. Peter was trimmin' my jibs
And was calling me home with my boots on
Smellin' like barbecued ribs!

Poor Jake took the blast a full frontal
Though his moustache protected his lips,
When he took his hat off his bald head,
He looked like a partial eclipse.

What kept us from burning too badly,
Or at least to me it makes sense,
Was the fireball of flammable gasses
Was mixed with the rumen contents.

The flames quickly waned to a flicker.
The cow was now layin' plum flat.
My chest was all greenish and sticky
. . . I could see by the light of my hat.

But the insult that cut me most deeply
Was not the burnt hat or the blood,
My mouth had been opened in protest!
And I found I was chewing her cud!

TILT TABLE VS. ROPING

Springtime. Grass is greenin' up, wildflowers are blooming, longjohns are comin' off, and it's brandin' time! It is a festive occasion on lots of ranches. For years it has become a time for neighbors to get together and help one another.

The cows and calves have been gathered the day before. By daylight horses have been unloaded, everybody's saddled up and the calves are sorted from their mamas. In the corral propane burners and branding pots are set up, brands heating, vaccine guns loaded, ear tags laid out, and dad's knife is sharp enough to clean a hornfly's fingernails!

Idyllic . . . right?

Wait . . . technology has reared its sleek, rancher's-helper automated-finger-mashing-clanging-banging-head, in the form of a tilt table calf squeeze chute!

So nowadays when your neighbor invites you to come help him brand his calves you mumble around. You're feeling him out as to whether he's still roping them and dragging them to the fire or pushing them through a long narrow alley, catching them in a calf chute and immobilizing the wiggling beasts. Sure, you appreciate that it's easier on the calves, the help, the horses, that it takes less time and labor, even less space than the traditional way, but it's so . . . mechanical, so feedlot, so farmerish. It's like work!

Branding calves is not supposed to be work! It's supposed to be like Christmas! The Fourth of July! Going to the National Finals Rodeo! Not like getting your Army physical or helping your neighbor unload a semi full of salt blocks. Ya dress up to come to a branding. You wear your chaps and your spurs, not your coveralls and steel-toed Redwings. You worry about missing your dally, not banging your head.

Getting run over in the alley lacks the excitement of having a calf run under your horse. A deft jab with a Hot Shot or professional SQ injection does not elicit the same 'Yee Haws' as a beautiful over-the-shoulder catch double hocking a snakey calf.

It's the difference between shooting a pheasant out of the air or hitting one with your car. Besides, it gives your horse a purpose, and you a little glamour. And we can all use that now and then.

Illustration: Don Gill

DADDY'S RANCH

I'm just sittin' here at my daddy's old desk
Just starin' out at the yard.
The barn looks the same as it always has,
I guess that's why it's so hard.

I can't put my finger on when it changed.
When you come back every year
You don't seem to notice that edges get round
And yer footprints disappear.

Machinery that once roamed this furrowed ground's
Evolved into dinosaurs.
The harness hangs empty, weary with age,
Cobwebs have covered the doors.

The fences are melting into the earth,
The trees are sixty feet tall
And here I sit in the afternoon sun
Tryin' my best not to bawl

'Cause here in my hand's an overdue note
With a letter in reply
You wrote him, Daddy, misspellings and all,
Beggin' more time to comply.

And another, a whole box full of bills
You're mortgaged up to the hilt!
A slave's what you were! Indentured and tied
To everything that you built

And you never said a word. All those times
Whenever we talked on the phone
Just, "How's the kids? Yep, yer Mama's okay,"
You had to do it alone.

Too proud? Too stubborn? Too afraid? I think
In the end it broke your heart.
If only you'd told me, I could have helped,
We'd gladly have done our part

To save the ranch. But as late as last week
We talked, you said things were fine.
The lawyer went over your books today...
'Sell out' was the bottom line.

I know why you did it. Too well I know.
To protect Mother and me.
I love the ranch, but this ranch is nothin'
Compared to you, don't you see.

You were my rock. And you always have been.
In my mind you hung the moon
And now when I need you the most, you're gone,
Oh, Daddy, you died too soon.

IT'S WHAT I DO

A cowboy is the way he is because he works with stock.
He's learned it's best to ease along
To find the rhythm in their song
And not to fret if days are long
'cause cows don't punch a clock.

That separates him from the crowd that keeps a job in town
That stack the boxes all in rows
Or bolt the knobs on radios
But when the evening whistle blows
they lay the hammer down.

"A job ain't done until it's done," that's life down on the farm.
To gather those who tend to stray
To treat the sick on Christmas Day
And if she needs your help, to stay.
Until she's safe from harm.

You see, you can't just quit a cow. Sometimes yer all she's got.
No reinforcements in the hall
No Nine-One-One to hear her call
Just you. Nobody else, that's all,
to get her through the spot.

His calling is as old as time. It is, will be and was.
Through blizzards, bogs and bob wire fence
He stands against the pestilence
And though he feigns indifference,
he's proud of what he does.

It's done without a second thought by those who tend the flock
"It's what I do," you'll hear them say
With no demand for higher pay
And I believe they are that way
because they work with stock.

CHAPTER 3

FEEDLOT, MARKET, BANKERS, BUSINESS, SHEEP

These subjects fall loosely under the term "livestock industry."

Feedlots are a specialized part of putting beef on the table. They receive new cattle (calves and growers) not unlike grade schools receive six year olds every fall. They come in large numbers and require constant attention for their first few months. Feedlot cowboys become experts in calf/child behavior. After immunizing new critters, they put them in first grade class and watch them daily to insure they learn to eat, drink and keep their elbows off the table.

At any sign of illness they are gently whisked by the first-responders to the in-house veterinary clinic where they are examined and treated appropriately. Depending on their incoming weight they will matriculate 4 to 6 months until they are graduated.

The affiliated industries that support agriculture, both plant and animal, play a huge part in the every day business of buying, caring for and selling the final product. It employs millions of people.

It may be compared to the airline business. Think how many are involved to support those who fly the plane.

And a word about sheep, wooley.

THE FAIRBOARD

It was every fairboard's nightmare
when the lightning hit the stage.
'Course, it might have been expected; it was just another page
In a trail of disasters that befell our county fair
That began when Dr. Knockwurst told us we should be aware

That a stomatitis outbreak might shut down the rodeo
Not to mention all the entries in the Junior Livestock Show.
Then the day before we opened they began to excavate
Down the center of the highway that runs up to the main gate.

Of course, they hit a waterline. We were Lake Louise by dawn.
But no water in the spigots in the barns or in the john.
So we planned on shuttle parking using pontoons and canoes
But we finally wound up asking folks to just take off their shoes.

And the carnival got testy 'cause we couldn't build a bridge
Plus the vendors all were grumblin' due to decreased patronage
But the tractor pull went okay
'cept they pulled a light pole down
Which played havoc with the dog trials
when two handlers almost drowned.

On the morning of the last night the promoter called to say
That the singer had a sore throat and could not perform, no way.
But by noon it didn't matter 'cause the clouds came rollin' in
And the crowd all left in lifeboats so by five we pulled the pin.

We retreated to the office down beneath the grandstand seats
Where the fairboard did its business
and hashed out the balance sheets.
'Cause tonight we were survivors. Like a pile of used retreads
Only glad that it was over, all we did was shake our heads

And ask ourselves why anyone would take this thankless chore
When a kid, in tow with mother,
stuck his head in through the door.
He had lost his yellow ribbon,
she explained, both drippin' pools,
And wondered if by some small chance,
if it weren't against rules...

94

Could we? "'Course we could!" I shouted.
"We're the fairboard! That's our thing!"
So we picked him out a dry one.
It was like we crowned him king.

And he tried to say his thank yous but his tears got in the way.
Time stood still as he departed. No one had too much to say
'Til the lightning hit the stage lights, then I heard me volunteer,
"I reckon we should get them fixed
'fore we do much else next year."

Illustration: Don Gill

SHEEPMEN, BORDER COLLIES AND MULES

What do sheepmen, border collies and mules have in common with cowboys, horses and blue heelers? Nothing, except they got off different ends of the bus when they got here.

Take mules, for instance. I don't think I've ever seen a stupid mule. But have you ever seen a sly, clever, vindictive, cantankerous, belligerent mule? Of course you have. That's why they get along with sheep people so well! Don't get me wrong, it's just that sheep people are practical and as long as they drag the camp and pack the pots and pans, they'll put up with a smart mule.

On the other hand the cowboy thinks you've got to show the mule who's boss. You don't show a mule who's boss. Mules are kinda like cats, they're just living at your place and doing as little as they can to stay there!

Horses, on the other hand are more frivolous creatures, which makes sheepmen uncomfortable. Matter of fact, fun in any form makes sheep people nervous. They've been at the bottom of the pecking order so long...the sheep people reading this are thinkin', "Oh, no, he's gonna tell one of those stupid sheep jokes." I'm not, not even the one about the ventriloquist.

But speaking of nervous, the border collie! One of the most amazing genetic creations on Earth. You can see them at dog trials. They are zipping back and forth like black and white hummingbirds, pucks on the ice, putting the sheep through the intricate obstacle course, and a lot of people think the sheep are in on it! They aren't!

And out standing in the corner of the field you see a person, a sheep person. You know it's a sheep person, 'cause, have you ever seen a cowboy standing out in the field? With a cane over his arm? No. Unless he's showing hogs at the fair.

As you become mesmerized by the almost telepathic communication between man and dog, you realize the time and effort it took to achieve this relationship; the endless training, the boring repetitive hours, on and on and on. But they both love it! They are serious as a root canal!

The cowboy, on the other hand, is not into dog training. Their relationship is sort of a "hike it to me and go out for a pass!"

96

Giving a good border collie to a cowboy like *moi* is like giving an 18 piece Taiwanese socket set to a cave man.

But every now and then you will see a sheepman go in the cow business or a cowman go in the sheep business and a mutant is formed. The sheep side of his brain keeps telling him, "Vote Republican, go to educational meetings, eat the heel, pay cash."

While the cowboy side of his brain is thinking, "I've got all my money in long term CDs, but I'd like something a little less risky...I think I'll buy a racehorse!"

CR

ONLY EWES CAN PREVENT WILDFIRES

Their motto is "Only ewes can prevent wildfire."

When I first heard about the Nevada Extension Service project involving sheep used in fire control, I had a momentary difficulty picturing the scene. Were they flying in low and dropping woolly beasts on hot spots? Were they fitting them with gas masks and shovels then parachuting lambs into the forest? Or were sheep serving some useful function at the base camp? Waiting tables, perhaps nursing wounds or simply offering comfort to the fire fighters in the form of a shoulder or fleece to lean on?

No! Of course not. The sheep simply eat everything in sight so nothing is left to burn.

Pretty clever, these Extension Service people. I understand they might apply for a grant to examine other alternative uses for sheep. I've come up with some possibilities they might test.

A replacement for the waterbed. Sleep on a 'Bed o' Sheep.' When trail riding or camping just bring 3 or 4 head along. They can reduce fire danger and you can count them at night.

How about soundproofing. When a teenager pulls up beside you in traffic and his Hi-Fi-whale communication car stereo is so loud it makes seismic waves in your 7-11 styrofoam cup, you can immediately dial 922-BRING-A-EWE. An emergency crew will be dispatched, arrive on the scene and stuff sheep inside the teen's car until the sound is properly muffled.

Or how about a safety device in automobiles to replace the airbag. In the event of a crash, a Bag O' Sheep explodes from the dash absorbing the impact then escapes out the broken windows.

Other things come to mind like a large drain stopper, a self-propelled sponge and a place to store your extra Velcro.

But the alternative use for sheep that may have the greatest potential; Q-tip for elephants.

ALL BEEF NUGGETS

There's been a significant trend toward larger cattle. Purebred breeders have concentrated their exotic genes 'til the modern bovine looks like a Great Dane on steroids. Much ado has been made about producing a leaner carcass. But the critters keep getting bigger. Maybe we're going the wrong way.

The object is to grow a product that will conform to the consumer's needs. Why not start breeding miniature cattle? The horse people have developed a miniature breed. Some of 'em are no bigger than a coon dog. Problem is, since you can't eat 'em, they're about as useful as pockets in yer underwear.

But imagine a herd of cattle so small you could keep 'em in a hat box. We're talkin' BITE SIZE!

Raisin' these miniature cattle would be a snap. They would forage in potted plants. You could run a couple thousand head in the backyard. When they were ready to go on feed, you could build 'em a ration outta corn flakes and shredded wheat.

At brandin' time you could invite the neighbors over. Everybody would get down on their hands and knees in the lawn and gather the herd into paper bags. You'd have to use your bifocals to earmark 'em. Cuttin' the bull calves would require the use of fingernail clippers and a good steady helper to hold their itty bitty legs.

You could haul 'em cross country in the back seat of a Buick. At the required rest stops, you could just turn 'em loose in the salad bar. The packin' house, as we know it, would become outdated.

98

Just clean 'em like a blue gill. Peel the hide and pop 'em in the freezer. Of course they'd be eaten 'bone in.' With all the emphasis on calcium in the diet, this should be a sales advantage. They'd be the perfect size for shish-kabobs and hot dog buns or dipped in guacamole as finger food. Fast food restaurants would be able to advertise pure WHOLE BEEF NUGGETS.

Finally, the sticky problem of waste disposal might beget the greatest financial boon of all. I've heard that people are makin' a killin' on microchips.

Illustration: Bob Black

99

COULD BE WORSE

The banker took his ledger out,
The rancher took a seat.
"Let's see, I lent you twenty thou
For cattle, corn and wheat.

"Let's talk about your cattle first."
The rancher's face looked pained.
"You know how bad the market's been.
Lost fifteen," he explained.

"Fifteen what? Fifteen cents a pound?
Fifteen died of thirst?"
"Nope, fifteen thousand dollars lost.
But, hey, it could be worse."

The banker swallowed hard then asked,
"Well, how about your grain?"
"The hoppers ate up all my wheat,
The sweet corn needed rain.

"The pigs got sick,   My son got drunk
And joined the Moonies church.
I figger I'm down forty thou
But, hey, it could be worse."

"Whataya mean, 'It could be worse!'
That ain't even funny!"
The rancher shrugged and then replied,
"Could'a been my money."

THE RANCHER AND THE BANKER

The rancher sat across the desk applying for a loan.
He'd never borrowed cash before, he'd made it on his own.
But times were hard, as he explained, and if they only could.
He'd like to borrow twenty grand. The banker understood.

"That doesn't sound unreasonable, although it's quite a lot.
Your cows can be collateral. How many cows you got?"
"Two hundred head," the rancher said,
"That's give or take a few."
"That's good enough," the banker said,
"Of course there's interest due."

In three months time the rancher came
and paid the loan in full
But in his poke he had some left that was expendable.
"Why don't you leave that cash with me,"
the banker said, content,
"You put your money in my bank and I'll pay ya eight percent,"

The rancher paused, "Now let me see...
you gave me twenty grand
And then I paid you extra back for lendin' me a hand.
Now I give you this pile of cash and you pay me this time
The extry that I done forked out, at slightly over prime?"

The banker nodded helpfully and lit himself a smoke.
The rancher seemed to cogitate and then he finally spoke,
"I ain't too good at high finance...you've put me on the spot
But fair is fair, so tell me, sir,
How many cows you got?"

LIVIN' IN TOWN

Livin' in town, boys, is hard, Lord, it's hard
Why, even the dog don't like the backyard.

I've spent all my life on the back of a horse
And that is a life I'd be glad to endorse

'Cept I've got a new baby, a kid startin' school
And it's tough to pay bills ridin' colts, packin' mules.

And so we gave notice and moved into town
But it's just for a while, 'til we get the down

To buy us a place to run a few cows
And a horse for the kid 'cause she ain't got one now.

A place where my wife can look up at the stars
Hear crickets and coyotes, not a chorus of cars

And I can go out in the cool evenin' air
And pee off the porch with no neighbors to care.

Maybe I'm dreamin', but dreamin's okay
They help an ol' cowboy to git through the day.

So I set on the couch after they've gone to bed
And hear the refrig as it hums in my head

And stare at the street light as sirens go by
Rememberin' when we came here and why.

I give my ol' brain some time to unwind
Knowin' tomorrow it's back to the grind.

I'll pet my ol' dog 'fore I turn out the light
He's wishin', like me, we wuz elsewhere tonight.

But for the time bein' our dreams have to wait
'Cause reality comes in the mornin' at eight.

THE REST OF US

He used to break horses, he used to herd sheep,
He worked in a feedlot awhile,
He grew up a'dreamin' he'd buy him a ranch
And raise horses and cattle in style.

But time pulled a fast one, life took a turn,
Dreams pulled the wool o'er his eyes,
'Cause it takes more than wishin' and workin' all day
To buy you a ranch and survive.

So now he sells saddles, or vaccine, or seed,
Or writes for the Livestock Gazette,
Doin' whatever it takes to stay close
To the land that he'll never get.

In ag economics or ranch real estate,
In his hat and his boots and his gloves,
Collectin' his check as he goes down the road
From the folks that he wishes he was.

Heck, he knows he's lucky to just have a job
That lets him stay close to his roots.
He may never own the ranch of his dreams
But at least he can pay for his boots.

Illustration: Don Gill

103

THE BARROOM DEAL

Sometimes the boss would make one of those "barroom deals." Like the time he bought Orby's cows.

Orby was one of yer genyoowine gypo cow traders and had injected a few loads of cows into us before.

Saturday morning, we gathered on a hill near the small town of Murphey. Orby brought along a couple of exchange students from Chihuahua to help.

Orby had built a temporary holding pen out of snow fence, chicken wire and steel posts. It looked like a concentration camp for discarded barnfowl. He'd rustled up some old panels and the first squeeze chute ever used by Thomas Jefferson. It was a Powder River squeeze and a Teco head gate. It was uniformly rust color and appeared to be held together by baler twine and botched welding beads.

The first cow clomped in and I put on a plastic sleeve to preg check her. "Whattya doin'" asked Orby. "Whattya think I'm doin', measurin' her for a monacle?" "They're all bred," he said, "My brother checked 'em last week. He kin tell by the way the hair lies on their spine."

The first one was open. As were the next seven. We worked for a couple hours, stoppin' to repair the chute twice. The cows were gettin' restless. Two of the boys stood on the ground between the chicken wire fence and the herd. They fended them off by shakin' a broken plastic whip and an empty Purina Dog Chow bag.

"This 'un's bound to be good." said Orby as he pushed a big, horned cow into the chute. She hit the head gate like a mortar shell just as I clamped the bar down over her neck. She never slowed down. She tore the head gate off and headed for the hills. The last time I saw her she was disappearin' over a creek bank followed by 172 head of "gar-on-teed" bovin reprobates. The head gate hung around her head like a picture frame. She was draggin' two miles of chicken wire, a 40-foot nylon rope and an empty bag of Purina Dog Chow.

The deal fell through. Sometimes we jes' git lucky.

THE CONSULTANT

Bein' in between jobs ain't no picnic.
In fact, it's downright insultant.
So I printed some cards, put signs in the yard,
And bingo, became a consultant!

I solicited quality rest stops
In search of the right clientele.
Passed out ballpoint pens to all of my friends,
Got an answer machine from Ma Bell.

At last an ol' timer sought my advice.
He brought in his last balance sheet.
I saw with a smile his management style
Was outdated and obsolete.

So I set out to solve all his problems.
I spoke like a preacher possessed!
He sat there amazed, his eyes sorta glazed,
I could see he was truly impressed.

He said not a word as I rambled on.
For effect, I went over it twice.
When time had expired, he politely inquired,
"How much for this expert advice?"

I said, "Fifty bucks." I thought it was fair.
From his looks I thought I could fake it.
But he nodded his head and finally said,
"Well, son, I don't think I'll take it!"

THE FEEDLOT MANAGER

Ah, the joys of upper management, of prestige and respect,
Making million dollar deals based on guts and intellect.
To co-ordinate production with disbursements every day,
His job, to run a feedlot and make that sucker pay!

He arrives to work at daybreak and drives around the yard.
Everything is peace and quiet, but his ulcer is on guard.
He's wary, but sees nothing to disturb the morning still
Then *WHOOMP!* From outta nowhere! An explosion at the mill!

The boiler's outta business! The welder's outta town!
But it doesn't make much difference
'cause the feed trucks 'er broke down!
So he clamors on the radio to get the cattle fed
But the feed boss is hungover and laid up home in bed.

The mill's still raining shrapnel! The feed bay is a mess
When the cattle foreman calls to say the calves are under stress.
They're backed up at the squeeze chute,
the hydraulic line froze tight!
And could he send an ambulance, there's been a little fight!

Then his secretary tracks him down to say she's got the flu,
There's cattle in the neighbor's yard, his margin call is due.
She said down at the stackyard somebody's spotted smoke
And up in pen one-seventeen the waterline is broke!

His wife called . . . from a public phone.
Her car won't start again,
The packer wants to wait a week to ship pens nine and ten.
In his office waiting patiently's the Pro-Biotics man
And a group of eager tourists on a field trip from Japan,

Plus the crew from 60 Minutes, his daughter's third grade class
And a roper needin' one day's work to buy a tank of gas.
So, one by one he handles it.
He screams and shouts and squawks
And pours himself a double shot of Maalox on the rocks!

Another day in management . . . another wooden horse.
It's no wonder he's incapable of social intercourse.

He's lived so long upon the razor's edge of the unknown
That he's not allowed in public view without a chaperone!

Now standing in the shambles of a mornin' shot to hell
His youthful expectations are exposed and bid farewell
By the motto of a manager who knows he's in his prime
That says, "Though everything's okay . . .
it's just a matter of time!"

THE FALL RUN

I was ridin' pens for Horton in the fall of '001.
It was in early October and the run had just begun.
He was buyin' calves like crazy 'cause the price was on the rise
And you couldn't see his pupils for the glitter in his eyes!

He bought big ol' soggy weaners . . .
soaked up virus like a sponge!
He bought dime-off little leppies
when the market made a lunge,
He bought Terramycin junkies that had been around the world
And hungry auction refugees
that stuffed their cheeks like squirrels!

He bought growers offa wheatgrass,
bought high mountain pasture calves,
He bought cuttin' bulls and ropin' steers,
the have-nots and the haves,
Bought heifers that were baggin' up
raised on leafy spurge and sage
And some that weighed two-fifty that were legal drinkin' age!

They were comin' in in boatloads!
Trucks were backed up gunwale deep
'Til the nightman up and quit us
'cause they wouldn't let him sleep!
It was busy as an anthill at Receiving every day,
Calves were standin' in the alley, in the bunk and in the way.

All awaiting to be processed by the ragged cowboy crew
Who'd begun to look like prisoners doin' hard time at the zoo!
I was horseback checkin' new ones
on the day before they broke
When the boss came drivin' up the bunk.
He stopped and lit a smoke,

Took a Tums and shot of Maalox,
blew his nose and spoke right out,
"Yessir, son," he said, *"This here's
what cattle feedin's all about!"*
It was several days before I chanced to see him after that
'Cause all hell broke loose next mornin'! I was in up to my hat!

It was more than just an isolated outbreak in the yard.
Any good luck we had goin' was completely au revoired!
Even "wreck" would understate it. Catastrophic comes to mind.
Like a hurricane, a bad divorce and toothache intertwined!

A four-alarm tub chopper fire! A dose of gas gangrene!
Then topped off with a napalm strike and scabies quarantine!
Chicken Little should'a been there!
He'da dang sure pooped his nest!
Every cowboy rode and doctored hardly gettin' any rest.

You can bet we earned our wages, kissed our one day off goodbye,
Workin' six o'clock 'til midnight, eatin' supper on the fly
'Til at last the plague just petered out . . .
Got gnawed down to the rind
And we've all got back to normal,
'cept the boss, who's now confined,

He's been checked into a clinic where they put 'im every year
To recover and rejuvenate and let his conscience clear.
Sort of, Jiffy Lube for managers who've lost their sense of place
Where they git their eyes reglittered and their memory erased!

Illustration: Charlie Marsh

EAT MORE BEEF!

I'm a fairly frequent victim of the
EAT MORE BEEF! campaign.
I've read the ads and seen the spots intended to explain
That if I will eat real beef, I will be real people
And have more iron inside me than a rusty Army Jeep'll!

It will make me thin and happy and put my life in order
And I agree in principle, I've been a staunch supporter.
But sometimes all this hoopelah just plain gives me the jitters.
See, I have a vested interest. I raised the blasted critters!

Which tends to make me cynical
to doubt or even scoff it.
'Cause from the cowman's point of view,
it ain't all fun and profit.
They've crippled more than one good horse
and countless good blue heelers,
An order buyer now and then, plus hordes of wheeler dealers.

And as for me, I've had my share of wounds and lacerations,
Of broken heads and swollen thumbs, unwelcome perforations.
They've knocked me down and knocked me out
and overhauled my keister
And woke me up on Christmas Day and kept me up 'til Easter!

They've embarrassed and ignored me, annoyed and misused me.
They've broke me flat as hammered pie,
they've mistreated and abused me,
And yet I keep on comin' back like bees keep makin' honey.
Maybe I'm a masochist 'cause it dang sure ain't the money!

So when they tell me EAT MORE BEEF!, I'll try and be attentive,
But tellin' me's a waste of time, I've got my own incentive.
I've spent a lifetime workin' cows which keeps a man believin'.
You bet yer life I EAT MORE BEEF! . . . I eat it to get even!

FOOD IS FOR PEOPLE, NOT PROFIT!

You've heard it said, no doubt, by those
Who study social digs,
"The 3rd World sits a starvin'
While we feed corn to pigs."

To those of you who think like that
You've got some noble goals.
Yet, your altruistic logic
Contains some gaping holes.

See, someone has to pay the bill
To grow the grain you want.
'Cause if we outlawed feeding pigs
And sold to government

The only way that Uncle Sam
Could get repayed at all,
Is sell that grain to governments
With backs against the wall

Who probably can't afford it,
'Cause if they could, ya know,
They wouldn't be in trouble now,
They'd bought it long ago!

You're generous, which I admire,
To wish to give away
The fruits of farmers' labors
To those who cannot pay.

Then you and I and Farmer Brown
Would each be taxed our share
To send our bounty overseas
Until our cupboard's bare.

Then we'd achieve your noble goal;
Equality...but listen,
What good is equal poverty
Without a pot...to stand on?

111

THE MARKER

The very first time I saw him, he was comin' off the truck.
The order buyer had averaged down or else,
just plain got stuck!
He went in a pen of feeders but when it came time to sell
The packer buyer cut him off. The reason rang a bell,

He looked like a long-haired Jersey! At least he did to me
And there might have been a camel somewhere in his family tree
'Cause he'd shed his hair in patches,
past the point of no return
Sorta like a shaggy carpet that somebody'd tried to burn!

So, he went with tailenders, got sorted off again
And made the rounds when springtime came
just goin' from pen to pen.
That summer he went out to grass
but he never gained a pound,
We vaccinated him that fall on his second time around.

The weeks drug on but I kept track,
in truth he was hard to miss,
'Cause he stuck out like a cold sore
on the lips you'd planned to kiss!

One day I told the foreman,
"Ya know, ol' Red's been here a while,
I figured his performance up and it's time to reconcile."
I calculated that he'd had six hundred days on feed,
Been through the chute so many times
he was almost broke to lead!

He had eaten sixteen thousand pounds of grain since he'd begun
And converted at a ratio of Two-Oh-Two to One.
Which, in fact is pretty sorry, unless you're raisin' whale,
So, that mornin' in the one-ton, ol' Red got shipped to the sale.

I was braggin' at the horse barn how I'd prob'ly get a raise
For pointing out that keepin' poor producers seldom pays.
Some of the boys objected, but sentiment has no place
In hard core ag economics, Red was a classical case.

The foreman cut my lecture short that evenin' just about five,
"Git yer butt down to receiving . . . time for the trucks to arrive."

New cattle were comin' from auctions,
local and countrywide.
When I went down to unload 'em,
I dang near laid down and cried!

Ol' Red come a'strollin' off the truck
like Caesar entering Rome.
He gimme sort of a "Gotcha" look
and said, "Hi, Honey, I'm home!"

Illustration: Don Gill

DUCK AND RUN OLYMPICS

When the crew came toward the cookhouse
Hazel shut and locked the door.
"Don't you even think about it!
Looks like y'all been in a war."

And though Hazel didn't know it
she was not that far off track
They'd been workin' pasture cattle
and them critters could fight back!

All that grass that they'd been eatin' lubricated their insides
Plus those cows were full as dog ticks and a little loose besides
So when squeezed in some tight corner
they could aim their guns at will
And bombard that crew of cowboys with recycled chlorophyll.

Now it's only grass and water as you'll hear the pundits say,
But I'm here to tellya, pardners, their performance on that day
Was a Duck and Run Olympics, a projectile Superbowl,
A team of Dutch boys at the dike who couldn't find the hole.

Willie got hit when his hot shot caught a big one by surprise.
With one long blast she turned him into split pea soup with eyes.
Big Sam looked like a seaweed when his beard took several shots
And Pedro's fancy brand new hat got covered with the trots.

A broadside fired from point blank range
went down O'Malley's shirt.
He emptied out the vaccine gun,
she matched him squirt for squirt.

Then Frank got trapped behind a gate
and watched with some concern
While the bunch backed up and measured him
and each one took a turn.

It was hangin' off their hat brim, it was drippin' off their clothes,
It was in their eyes, in their ears and prob'ly up their nose.
Not a cowboy was untainted, not a dog escaped the muck,
Not a standin' stick, a saddle horse, a whip or chute or truck

Was immune to their propellant. They resembled works of art,
Little guacamole statuettes or cow pie ala carte.
Hazel backed'em to the spigot and stood beside the trough,
"I can't clean up your cowboy ways, but I'll hose the outside off."

Sam was lookin' at O'Malley, "Is this what they really mean
When an Irish cowboy celebrates the wearin' of the green?"
"I don't think so," said O'Malley, "but when I see cows eat grass
I'll forever be reminded of that phrase, *'this too shall pass.'"*

THE MAPLE CREEK OPEN

The scene was the annual stockdog trials
At Maple Creek, Saskatchewan,
All the sheepmen for miles had come for the trials
And brought a dog he would matchewan.

Then a stranger pulled up to the fence,
"New Meat" the locals were hopin',
From the back of his truck he drug out ol' Tuck
And entered him up in the Open.

The Open was after the Novice,
The good dogs all put on a show,
They were reachin' and stretchin', liftin' and fetchin'
And givin' each other a go!

Then last but not least came ol' Tuck
And he did right well, 'til the end
And he woulda done better, if he'd quit when he shed'er,
But he ate the last ewe that he penned!

I mean, right there in front of the judge!
Just like a boa constrictor!
He looked happy indeed as he spit out a seed*
And savored the spoils of the victor.

"Disqualified!" screamed the contestants,
Their objections were loud and profane,
Tuck watched all the while with his lanolin smile
While his master begged time to explain.

"I see that wee Tuck has offended
With his indiscriminate zeal
I regret his bad taste but no one's disgraced,
So he ate an ol' ewe...no big deal!

"Lord knows I've tried to teach him good manners
But you've got to admit that ol' sheep
Was tough as a shoe an' dang hard to chew
But Tuck never complained... not a peep!

"I'm sorry he partook yer pore darlin'
He did only what he thought was right
From tail to head, he's Canadian bred,
He ate her to just be polite!"

*Sheep have little seeds, ya know. You see 'em scattered all over the
ground wherever sheep are.

116

ANIMAL LOVERS

Let's talk about animal lovers
Not those who protest and accuse
But everyday people who carry the load
And don't make the six o'clock news.

It's proper to make the distinction
When explanations are given;
Between those who care as a hobby
And others who care for a livin'.

When we speak of animal lovers
The part-time groups come to mind.
Nice enough folks, who articulate well,
And shine when the cameras grind.

It's too bad more credit's not given
To the ones who seldom get heard
'Cause, in spite of their modest behavior,
Their actions speak louder than words.

These are the folks that on Christmas Day
Take care of God's animals first
With never a thought they should have the day off
Or that they might be reimbursed.

They believe that Genesis meant it,
That man has dominion o'er all,
And they don't take their mandate too lightly
To care for the great and the small.

God's entrusted His creatures to us
By rating us all in His log
According to what our abilities are;
Most get a house cat or dog.

But the bulk of the animal kingdom
He placed in the hands of a few
Who feel more at home in a pasture than
An office on Fifth Avenue.

God did it that way for a reason
'Cause talk's cheap where carin's concerned.
The title of animal lover is
An honor that has to be earned.

To those who'd debate my conclusion
To your own you're welcome to cling.
But I'll bet if we'd ask His opinion
God knows that He did the right thing.

BORDER COLLIE SOLILOQUY

Just a word about one of the greatest genetic creations on the face of this earth . . . the border collie.

Faster than a speeding bullet! More powerful than a locomotive. Able to leap tall fences in a single bound!

The dog that all sheep talk about but never want to meet. The fur that legends are made of. Makes coyotes cringe, sheep trip the light fantastic and eagles soar somewhere else.

Invested with the energy of a litter of puppies, the work ethics of a boat person and the loyalty of Lassie, they ply their trade on sagebrush flats, grassy fields and precipitous peaks from sea to shining sea.

"Away to me!" I command. They streak and sail, zipping like pucks upon the ice. Black and white hummingbirds, in, out, up, down, come by.

Sheep. With head up, one eye cocked over their shoulder asking directions. To the gate through the race. Mighty dog moves behind the bunch like a towboat pushing barges around a bend.

And heart. Do they try? *"Just let me at'em, Dad!"* Stay! *"C'mon, I'm ready!"* Stay! *"Can't you feel me hummin'! Listen to my heart! It's purrin' like a cat! I am primed! Aim me, point me, pull the trigger!"*

"Away to me!" It makes me feel like Robin Hood. He leaves my side like an arrow.

Workin' dogs is like manipulating a screwdriver with chopsticks. Like doing calligraphy with a plastic whip. Like bobbing for apples. Like threading a needle with no hands. Like playing pool on the kitchen table.

There are no straight lines in nature. Only arcs. Great sweeping curves of sight and thought and voice and dog. Always having to lead your command about a dog's length.

Sheep bunched like logs on the river. Dogs paddling in the current, always pushing upstream. A ewe breaks loose. Then another, another. The log jam breaks. Dogs and sheep tumble about in the white water.

Calm again, they start back upstream.

Border collies. Are they truly smarter than a chimpanzee? Cuddlier than a koala? More dedicated than Batman's valet?

Can they change course in mid air? Drag Nell from the tracks and locate the missing microfilm?

Yes. I believe they can. They are the best of the best, the epitome of 'above and beyond the call of duty.' Head Dog. Top Gun. I salute you, for man has never had a better friend.

Illustration: Charlie Marsh

119

OLD BLUE

I loved ol' Blue
as much as a man
could love
a man's best friend

And when his time came
I helped him along
I owed him that much
in the end.

❧

COWBOY CONFUSION

At times a cowboy's lingo can result in some confusion.
Which brings a clash of cultures to a head.
Mo and I were breedin' heifers, artificially, of course,
By five we got the last one finally bred.

We headed into Vera's place for supper and a brew.
To our surprise a crowd stood in the street.
For tomorrow they had scheduled an Olympic Field Day
And all the locals hankered to compete.

They'd selected the officials but they needed volunteers
'Cause all the jobs weren't filled as they desired
So they canvassed the assemblage seeking suitable recruits
And cornered Mo and graciously inquired

In the women's cycling contest, would he consent to be a judge?
Mo swallowed hard and gave his beer a quaff.
Said he, somewhat embarrassed, "I doubt I'm qualified, besides,
I'm sure I can't get twenty-eight days off!"

120

FLYNT & FRANK

Dear Bax,

Flynt and I can't tell you how much we enjoyed your visit. It was sure nice of y'all, especially with that bad cold. Even though both kids caught it from you, so far only one has gone into pneumonia.

Flynt thought it was sure great that you castrated all our colts while you were here. Although neither one of us had ever seen quite that much blood, at least we didn't have to wonder what happened when we found eight of them dead the next morning. Flynt got real excited once I explained to him how much money we were saving by only having to feed two head instead of ten. Not only that, the two that survived sure look like money makers once we get them over the tetanus.

Remember when we were sitting in that bank president's office and you were telling how all the smart bankers out west were calling in their unstable cow notes? Well sir, you won't believe this but that banker thought that was such a good idea that he's doing the exact same thing here. By not having any cows to feed or interest to pay there's no telling how much money we'll save this year.

And Baxter, I don't want you worrying about backing into the carport and knocking it down. In the first place, it's hard to stop any type of vehicle going 55 mph in reverse and secondly, as you remember, Beverly only had that one big gash over her eye when we lifted the roof off her.

Flynt was just commenting the other day about how times sure did get away from us while you were here. All of a sudden we looked up and 6 weeks and 5 days had just whizzed by. We were sure sorry to see you go but since our livestock was about depleted and a good portion of our standing structures leveled I guess it was as good a time as any. Oh, by the way, the folks from the car rental place came by and picked up the Lincoln and were kind enough to set us up on a monthly payment plan until the $6300 in mileage and damages were paid off.

As Always,

Flynt and Frank

THE SUPERSALESMAN

Slicker'n deer guts on a doorstep! Smooth as a filly's nose!
Here in this jug's a miracle drug so new that nobody knows!
Feed it, inject it or plant it, stick it under an ear.
Pick any breed, results guaranteed, the data's perfectly clear.

It's good for footrot in gophers, chafing on buffalo thighs,
Horses with corns, Angus with horns
And girls with fire in their eyes!
Goats with a bad disposition, lovers losing their spark,
Turpentined cats, blindedfolded bats
And dogs that forgot how to bark!

Friends, Are you troubled with aphids?
Kids all down with the flu?
Cattle won't gain? Needing more rain? I tellya what this'll do;
Kill all the weeds in your garden, patch up an innertube,
Leaven your bread, stiffen your thread
And work out your Rubik's cube!

Give you more miles per gallon, relieve your gastric distress,
If that ain't enough, this wonderful stuff
Eats barbecue stains off yer dress!
I see you don't quite believe me! The best I saved for last.
Pay me the cash then quick as a flash! See? Oh, I went too fast.

Okay, let's do it again,
Watch and you'll understand.
Safe and improved, it gently removes
A five dollar bill from your hand!

Illustration: Bob Black

TO THE FEEDLOT HOSS

Boys, I offer a toast
To that creature tied to the post
Who through all his ills and occasional spills
Still gives us more than his most

He's black, bay or he's brown
Sorrel or spotted around
He eats that ol' hay even cows throw away
And makes his bed on the ground

'Round machinery and pumps that paddle
And trucks and gates that rattle
By a mill that roars he does his chores
He come here to jis' punch cattle

See them four brands on his side
The ones that wuz burnt in his hide
He's been around and covered more ground
Than we'd ever care to ride

For beauty he's often hard put
Covered with mill dust and soot
But in a slick pen or a mud and snow blend
He'll go where you won't go afoot

In dust so thick you can't see
He breathes the same air that you breathe
And in cold rain he feels the same pain
That numbs and stiffens your knees

When the sun's beatin' down on yer head
And the rest of the day lies ahead
He's dreamin' too of the ranch he once knew
Where green grass and shade make a bed

Yup, he makes every step that you take
And feels each ache that you ache
And sweats, two fer one every drop that you run
And seldom asks for a break

So before you mount up and start
Think of yer four-legged pard
When he seems short on brains jus' give him the reins
'Cause boys, he's durn long on heart

CHAPTER 4
HORSES, RODEO, VETERINARIANS

In the wonderful world of cowboys, the horse is an essential tool. It has evened the odds in the COW vs COWBOY equation. A cowboy without a horse is like a rope without a loop, a battleship without a gun, or a fire-eater without a match.

Most horses are dignified and strong, everything is measured in horsepower. They are inspirational, trustworthy and heroic. How would Roy Rogers, Robert E. Lee, the Man from Snowy River, Ghengis Khan, Billy Etbauer and the Cisco Kid be remembered without their magnificent steed? They lend glamour and power to whomever has them as a partner.

The horse has played many parts on the big stage of mankind, from pulling Egyptian chariots, to conquering the Trojans, to carrying Crazy Horse over the Little Big Horn, and to taking World Champion Rodeo cowboy Trevor Brazile on the ride of his life.

Horse people are a breed of their own. It is often a weakness ... the need to have horses in their world, even if they serve no obvious purpose.

As Clyde Ridgeway once said, "I'd walk a mile to saddle horse to go a half a mile."

My chosen profession, veterinary medicine, is referenced as far back as 300 BC. In the first chapter of the book of Genesis, cattle are one of the first creatures God gives Adam dominion over.

We have progressed through the centuries to veterinary diagnostic and treatment procedures that are virtually "Star Wars" technology! Yet, even today, vets with ten years of college education find themselves with a bucket of water and a bar of soap standing in front of a 50 pound uterine prolapse that is actually glaring up at them with the same malevolence as one of Moses's heifers might have done!

We go back a long way.

LEGACY OF THE RODEO MAN

There's a hundred years of history and a hundred before that
All gathered in the thinkin' goin' on beneath his hat.
And back behind his eyeballs and pumpin' through his veins
Is the ghost of every cowboy that ever held the reins.

Every coil in his lasso's been thrown a million times
His quiet concentration's been distilled through ancient minds.
It's evolution workin' when the silver scratches hide
And a ghostly cowboy chorus fills his head and says, "Let's ride."

The famous and the rowdy, the savage and the sane
The bluebloods and the hotbloods and the corriente strain
All knew his mother's mothers or was his daddy's kin
'Til he's nearly purely cowboy, born to ride and bred to win.

He's got Buffalo Bill Cody and Goodnight's jigger boss
And all the brave blue soldiers that General Custer lost
The ghost of Pancho Villa, Sittin' Bull and Jessie James
All gathered by his campfire keepin' score and takin' names.

There's every Royal Mountie that ever got his man
And every day-work cowboy that ever made a hand
Each man that's rode before him, yup, every mother's son
Is in his corner, rootin', when he nods to make his run.

Freckles Brown might pull his bull rope,
Casey Tibbs might jerk the flank,
Bill Pickett might be hazin' when he starts to turn the crank.
Plus Remington and Russell lookin' down his buckhorn sight
All watchin' through the window of this cowboy's eyes tonight.

And standin' in the catch pen or in chute number nine
Is the offspring of a mountain that's come down from olden time
A volcano waitin' quiet, 'til they climb upon his back
Rumblin' like the engine of a freight train on the track.

A cross between a she bear and a bad four-wheel drive
With the fury of an eagle when it makes a power dive
A snake who's lost it's caution or a badger gone berserk
He's a screamin', stompin', clawin', rabid, mad dog piece o' work.

From the rollers in his nostrils to the foam upon his lips
From the hooves as hard as granite to the horns with dagger tips
From the flat black starin' shark's eye that's the mirror of his soul
Shines the challenge to each cowboy like the devil callin' roll.

In the seconds that tick slowly 'til he climbs upon his back
Each rider faces down the fear that makes his mouth go slack
And cuts his guts to ribbons and gives his tongue a coat
He swallows back the panic gorge that's risin' in his throat.

The smell of hot blue copper fills the air around his head
Then a single, solid, shiver shakes away the doubt and dread
The cold flame burns within him 'til his skin's as cold as ice
And the dues he paid to get here are worth every sacrifice

All the miles spent sleepy drivin', all the money down the drain
All the "if I's" and the "nearly's," all the bandages and pain
All the female tears left dryin', all the fever and the fight
Are just a small downpayment on the ride he makes tonight.

And his pardner in this madness that the cowboys call a game
Is a ton of buckin' thunder bent on provin' why he came
But the cowboy never wavers he intends to do his best
And of that widow-maker he expects of him no less.

There's a solemn silent moment that every rider knows
When time stops on a heartbeat like the earth itself was froze
Then all the ancient instinct fills the space between his ears
'Til the whispers of his phantoms are the only thing he hears

When you get down to the cuttin' and the leather touches hide
And there's nothin' left to think about,
he nods and says, "Outside!"
Then frozen for an instant against the open gate
Is hist'ry turned to flesh and blood, a warrior incarnate.

And while they pose like statues in that flicker of an eye
There's somethin' almost sacred, you can see it if you try.
It's guts and love and glory - one mortal's chance at fame
His legacy is rodeo and cowboy is his name.

"Turn 'im out"

JOHNNY WAS A MULE MAN

Johnny was a mule man, which says a lot to me.
His motto: keep it simple. Lay it out for me to see.
If a kid can't understand it, it's pro'bly bound to fail.
He'd rather have a good man's word than a contract in the mail.

He never trusted horses or computers on the the shelf,
He'd rather count the cattle, check the pasture for himself.
If he knew you knew your business, he'd back you to the hilt
And gladly give the credit for the fences that you built.

But he'd ride you like a blanket so you couldn't go astray
'Cause to him it all was pers'nal . . . he knew no other way.
He didn't have the answers to each problem you were heir
But he figgered you could solve'em. That's why he put you there.

If you could tie a diamond hitch or pour the ol' concrete
That meant as much to him as runnin' out a balance sheet.
See, he knew that all the business
in the end came down, somehow
To a single salaried cowboy who went out and checked a cow.

I guess he always thought himself not one of the elite
But a man who works for wages and just got a better seat.
And I'm sure he spent some sleepless nights
doubting what he'd done
But he trusted his opinion more than almost anyone's.

So, if he prayed, which most men do, when sleep is closing in,
He pro'bly prayed that Scottish prayer that suited men like him,
"Lord, grant that I am right, that my judgment's not gone blind.
For Thou knowest in Thy wisdom, it's hard to change my mind."

The life lessons I learned from Johnny Basabe;

1) How to win the game when you don't know the rules.
2) How to find your way when you don't have a map.
*3) And, when someone tells you it can't be done, what
they mean is 'they can't do it.'*

THE GRAPEVINE

How better to impress his new lady friend, thought Rob, than to take her to his friend's rancho for an afternoon branding and BBQ.

She would be pleased to see that he had many friends who drove pickups with chrome grills guards, tinted windows and coordinated paint jobs. He admitted to himself that his own outfit was less ostentatious. His '84 model two horse trailer had been repaired so many times that it looked like a well drillin' rig! The '96 pickup was using 2 qts of oil to a tank of gas and his horse was . . . well, ol' Yeller looked right at home.

Rob was eager as a piddlin' puppy when he picked up Delilah and headed north outta the Los Angeles area. He was anxious to make a decent impression but one large obstacle lay in the pit of his stomach like a pea in the Princess's mattress . . . THE GRAPEVINE! It was a monster of a hill dreaded by truckers and people who still drove compact cars.

The engine was screamin' and smokin' like a burnin' pile of creosote posts when they finally leveled out at the summit of the Grapevine. Rob had sweated through his shirt but he sighed with relief as he gave Delilah a comforting look. She smiled back uneasily. Then the motor blew! A big dent appeared in the hood and it sounded like someone had dropped a Caterpillar track into the fan!

They coasted silently into a service station at the bottom of the grade. He assured his sweetheart there was *"no problema"*. He had lots of friends nearby. Her reaction was one of forced optimism.

By dark he'd borrowed a pickup from Hank and they both agreed returning back home was the best option. He loaded Yeller, hooked up the trailer and back over the Grapevine they flew! Halfway down Rob managed to slip his arm behind Delilah's neck. Soon she was lulled into discussing her dreams of home and family. She snuggled closer as he watched a tire bounce by him on the driver's side. No headlights shown in his rearview but he couldn't help but notice the huge rooster tail of sparks spraying up from beneath his trailer! He could see her astonishment in the flickering light.

129

Rob wheeled the screeching rig to the shoulder! Together they unwired the trailer doors and Yeller stepped out, unhurt. Rob tied him to the highway fence and unhooked the trailer. Rob's facial tic had returned.

Seemingly in control, he jumped in the pickup and headed south for the nearest phone to borrow a trailer. He returned to the scene to find Yeller grazing in the median with semis whizzing by on both sides and his date, shivering, over the still warm axle, forgotten. She, herself, was smoldering. She spoke not a word and Rob conceded to himself that it was gonna be hard to regain her confidence.

In the space of 12 hours and 50 miles he had left his pickup, his trailer, his horse and his girl scattered from one end of the Grapevine to the other.

Next day he towed the pickup to the shop. He left his trailer to be impounded by the State Police. His horse made it home safe but Delilah changed her phone number, wrote him out of her will and had not been heard of since!

CR

COOP DE GRACE

"Well, at least it isn't broken," *he said as he wiped his face*
With his good arm. "Although it might be a smidgen outta place.
That sucker sure did buck hard! I'm glad I was wearin' my hat
Or I'da punched right through that net wire fence
and hung there like a bat!

Dadgummit! Where's the rest of my shirt?
All but the sleeves are gone!
And my chest has got a pattern you could make a waffle on!
I remember him a'squallin' with my collar in his teeth
As I flopped from neck to shoulder
like a rubber Christmas wreath!

Have ya seen my other batwing leg? I had it, I'da sworn.
I never wear just half a pair. Musta hooked it on the horn
When he ran it up my pantleg where my inseam used to be!
And my off hind boot is missin'! Heck, that don't bother me,

130

It could still be in the stirrup 'cause I had a deadman's grip!
I made several revolutions from his belly to his hip,
Checked the bosal and the back cinch as I orbited around!
He pumped me like a plumber plungin' dirty water down!

Then bounced me off the buckin' rolls
when he went to changin' gears!
I did a back flip and catapulted out between his ears
But I hung tight to the neck rein as I spun and ricocheted
Like someone tied a chicken to a helicopter blade!

I was airborne several minutes 'fore I landed in a heap
And, exceptin' for this hatband there ain't nothin' left to keep!
Can't remember if he kicked me but these tracks are livin' proof,
This here trademark on my pocket looks suspiciously like hoof.

Don't know how the sucker bucked me off.
It happened way too fast
But nobody has to tell this fool that I been coop de grassed!
It's a story old as cowboys and sometimes the horses win
But, at least it isn't broken, so best catch'im up again!"

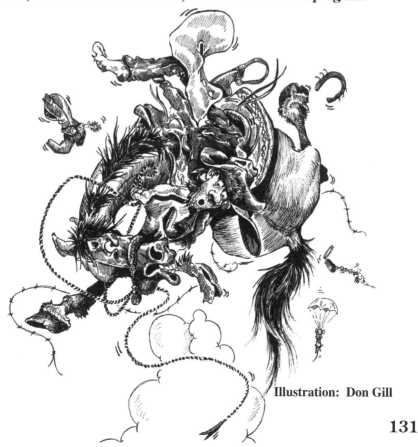

Illustration: Don Gill

131

THE PRACTITIONER'S LOT

Today in the world of modern vets
I've lost my place in line
My colleagues have prospered as specialists
In therio or swine.

I see their achievements in magazines,
Their articles are in print.
They've developed a cure for seedy warts
With after dinner mints

Or they're recognized as the final word
In matters so complex
That I can't pronounce what they're working on
Much less, what it affects!

I spend my days at the back of a cow
Usually up to my chin
In the process of pullin' somethin' out
Or pushin' it back in!

Or I'm tryin' to pass a catheter
To move a calculi
While the cat is tearin' my arm to shreds
And sprayin' my good tie!

I dream to discover a new technique
But it's not meant to be.
The chances are slim that they'd even name
A prolapse after me!

But I'm thankful I've got a good practice
With loyal clientele
Who, in spite of my vast shortcomings, still
Try and speak of me well.

Why, just last week two farmers were talkin'
Outside my clinic door
"Doc ain't perfect, but for our little town
We couldn't ask for more."

"Yea, I'll agree," the second one answered,
"I've given it some thought,
With Doc you always git yer money's worth
But . . . he don't charge a lot!"

HE WAS OK YESTERDAY

"Doc, I called you just as soon
as I seen ol' Buck was sick.
He's been a little poorly
But he never missed a lick.

Last winter he got picky
And wouldn't eat his grain
So I gave him Doctor Bell's;
Tied garlic in his mane.

Then several months ago
When he started losin' weight
I give him Copenhagen
And a pound of catfish bait.

He come down with the splatters
And all his hair fell out!
So I fed him Larramycin
And Mother's sauerkraut.

Then last week after ridin'
He got as stiff as pine!
His navel needed smokin'
So I used the turpentine.

He went plum down on Sunday.
His kidneys, so I guessed.
I doctored up his water
And tied him facin' west.

Last night I got to thinkin',
You were here two years ago.
You gave him some concoction
For a cough and runny nose.

I wondered if your treatment,
Which then improved his luck,
Had later turned against him
And poisoned my ol' Buck?

Whattya think, Doc?"

"DOC, WHILE YER HERE . . ."

Doc, sorry I called so late but you must be all through eatin'.
I appreciate you comin' out. Yer truck shore took a beatin'
   On my gravel road but I swear I'll get it graded.
I know I promised last time, but all this mud delayed it.

The cow's up in the pasture. I should'a called you sooner
But after lunch I took a nap, what Mama calls a nooner.
I read the mail and fed the dog and sat around and thought
Then I watched ONE LIFE TO LIVE, and Doc, I plum forgot.

Sorry 'bout this busted chute. I tried to get a welder.
But last time I used baler twine and I'm pretty sure it held'er.
   I'm glad you brought a flashlight.
   This bulb's been out since May.
I'll have it fixed the next time I call you out this way.

   Water? You mean drinkin' water?
   There's some in that old barrel.
But a rat drowned in there Tuesday so I'd be a little careful.
Oh, I just remembered, the kid's ol' Shetland pony
Got in a sack of barley and now he's actin' groany.

And since yer here already, the dog ain't had his shots.
The hogs got diarrhea and I've been seein' spots.
If it's not too much to ask, would you use these pills I bought.
   They're cheaper at the Co-op,
   Doc, you charge more than you ought.

I thank y'all fer comin', Doc, you've treated me alright.
I told the wife to call you first, especially late at night.
If you ever need a reference, I'll put you in my will
And about tonight's expenses . . . Just put it on my bill.

Illustration: Don Gill

THE VET'S WIFE'S REFRIGERATOR

A scream from the kitchen. The thud of a faint.
She sighs and arises and walks with restraint.
Her neighbor lays peaceful, eyes fixed in a stare
She's passed out in front of the new Frigidaire.

She looks at the rack with eggs in its keep
Winking up at her's the eye of a sheep.
There's a bottle of PenStrep near the Swanson's pot pies
And down in the crisper's a bag full of flies.

The butter tray's filled with test tubes of blood
Marked, E.I.A. samples, from Tucker's old stud.
High on the shelf near a platter of cheese
is a knotted, but leaking, obscene plastic sleeve.

Fecal containers are stacked, side by side,
With yesterday's pieces of chicken, home fried.
The freezer's a dither of guts, lungs and spleens
Scattered amongst the Birds Eye green beans.

Her home's a museum of animal parts.
Lymphomatous lymph nodes, selenium hearts.
Enough tissue samples to hold up a bridge
But why do they always end up in the fridge?

But she doesn't worry or turn up her nose,
She's the wife of a vet, it's the life that she chose.
But maybe he'd worry at lunch if he knew
He might just be dining on Whirl-Pack stew!

THE UTAH COWBOY

He was a Utah cowboy and he wore a big felt hat
That was pulled down level to his ears
till the tops of them were flat.
The weathered lines upon his face showed
he had a checkered past
I reached to shake his proffered hand
but both his wrists were in a cast!

"Carpal tunnel?" I asked deadpan but he never broke a grin.
"Rodeo," he quietly said. "Bulls or broncs?" I asked again.
"No. Team roping," was his answer.
I responded, "Quite a wreck?"
"Well, the heeler saw it better,"
then he winced and stretched his neck

And then began his tragic tale, "I was on my trader horse
Who hadn't bucked for ne'r two weeks
and was steady on the course.
You know how you have always thought
if yer dallied up and tight,
A horse can't buck while draggin' all that weight?
Well, pardner, that ain't RIGHT!

"My heeler's horse came off the ground
when my pony broke in two!
The second jump we cleared the fence
but I held my dallies true.
The third time like a slingshot put the poor ol' steer in orbit
And I'm thinkin', 'If I make this ride
I might get a good score,' but

He fired me from the saddle with such force he come unshod,
And bucked so hard up to the sky, so high that I saw God.
Brigham Young was there beside him, according to this spiel,
Respectfully I waited for some wisdom he'd reveal;

Some divine sent revelation of man's purpose here on Earth,
Or a glimpse of cowboy heaven, or what angels' cows are worth."
"Did he give you any inkling of your future, dirt to dirt?"
"Yes, he did," the cowboy whispered,
"He said, 'Son, this is gonna hurt.'"

he sang...
'little Joe the wrangler'

Illustrated by
Dave Holl

The dry grass crackled underfoot,
was dang near stirrup high
The horse and rider left a wake
as they went riding by
Their shadow swam beneath
the horse, no elbows stickin' out
The hoppers thick as dirt road dust,
the prairie sick with drought

No cattle in this section piece. They stayed down by the creek
The rider only rode to see how bad it was this week
Due east across the grassy sea he rode with squinting eyes
No cloud to break the baking heat, but then to his surprise

The slightest shadow fell across the ground on either side
He stirred from somnolescent thought, from soporific ride
His senses came alert and he sat straighter in the seat
The blue sky had a pinkish tinge . . . and then he felt the heat

He swung his horse back to the west and saw the wall of flame
The god of fire was hot to trot and back to stake its claim
It felt like his whole head caved in
as blood drained from his brains
The fist of fear that gripped his heart
squeezed dread into his veins

They wheeled as one and in two jumps were flying 'cross the plain
They ran flat out for near a mile but hardly did they gain
For now the fire was like a mob that fed upon its own
Self-conflagrating cannibals cremating flesh and bone

The smoke was in his horse's nose,
the fear was in his eyes
The froth blew off his heaving
flanks and soon was vaporized
A hole, a hump, a hidden clump,
whatever . . . jammed the gear
The horse went down like he'd
been shot
The rider landed clear

138

The flames hung down like curtains there behind the fallen horse
The beast was struggling to his feet, the wind was gaining force
The rider dug a wooden match from out his sweaty shirt
And struck it on his zippered fly, then reached down to the dirt

And lit a clump of tinder grass without a second thought
In moments with the steady breeze the helpless prairie caught
The horse in panic tried to run but couldn't bear his weight
His right hind packed up under him. The rider didn't wait

He peeled his shirt off with a tug and quickly tied a blind
Around the faunching horse's head to try and calm his mind
The spot he'd lit was fanning out but in its wake lay bare
A blackened smoking patch of ground that beckoned to the pair

With coaxing-pulling-pounding will, he danced the horse around
Until they stumbled through the ring
and stood on burnt-off ground
He jerked his rope down from the horn and, talking all the time
He sidelined up the good hind foot to drop him on the dime

Then pulled him down and dallied up
and somehow with the rest
Reached down and looped the left front foot
and pulled it to his chest
He looked up at the raging fire that towered overhead
The wind that beat hard on his face
now pressed his back instead

The fire was sucking oxygen to feed its hungry forge
The backdraft fueled the dragon's flame
that bore down on St. George
With nylon rope and reins in hand
the rider cuddled near
He lay beside the stricken horse
and sang into its ear

...*He's Little Joe the wrangler, boys*...the fire became a roar
It rose up like a cobra's hood...*he'll wrangle never more*...
The sky turned black...*An OK spur from one foot lightly hung*...
The devil's furnace set on high but still the cowboy sung

...*The boss he cut him out a mount*...like bugs caught in a yawn
They lay in the volcano's throat...*and kindly put him on*...
Surrounded by a ring of fire, they clung to their domain
Two captives on a railroad track beneath a passing train

...*He's ridin' ol' Blue Rocket with a slicker o'er his head*...
The peak of the inferno was enough to wake the dead
The rider tugged the shirt on down to wrap the horse's nose
His voice raw, he whisper-sang and kept his own eyes closed

...*But one of us was missin', boys*...by now he'd worn a groove
Together there, just mouth to ear the pony never moved
...*Next mornin' just at daybreak*...then the wind began to turn
The rider felt a different breeze, his cheeks began to burn

...*Beneath him mashed into a pulp*...still trapped in his own hell
The rider croaked his scraping dirge...
His spur had wrung the knell...
How long he held the horse's head
no one could really know
And on he sang...*Our little Texas
stray poor Wrangler Joe*...

The pilot finally spotted them and radioed the ground
The boys who reached him in the truck
weren't sure what they had found
The horse was layin' on his side his head a'pointin' north
The rider hunkered over him just rockin' back and forth

The tee shirt burnt clean off his back, his bare head fairly scorched
The horse's hair was singed like wool, his mane and tail torched
The pair smelled like a brandin' fire but what disturbed the boys
Was comin' from the rider's lips, a scratchy humming noise

A raspy ragged lullaby that carried on the air
And slithered up their prickled necks and held 'em frozen there
Before them grinned the face of death, the Earth, its skin unpeeled
The world consumed by fire this time, Apocolypse revealed

But beating in this ruined place two hearts somehow prevailed
And hung in balance by a thread...a sigh could tip the scales
Then Jim eased up, like you would do a spooky colt, perhaps
And touched him with an outstretched hand...
the rider just collapsed

This tale was told in countless camps
where killin' time's the rule
Some say the rider was insane
and babblin' like a fool
But Jim, who reached the rider first
was haunted his life long
With *Little Joe the Wrangler...*
But, who knows...it's just a song.

VETERINARY DIAGNOSTIC VOICE MAIL

Hello. You have reached the automated voice mail of <u>Triple A,</u> <u>Aardvarks Are Us, All Creatures Great and Small Veterinary</u> <u>Clinic, Animal Health Supply, Grooming, Boarding, Training,</u> <u>and Counseling Center.</u> *If you have a credit card limit of no less than five thousand dollars please press one, if not please hold.*

[1] Thank you. If your problem concerns a pet - including dogs, cats, small rodents, reptiles, cockatiels, highway accidents and other creatures where cost is no object, please press one.

If you have livestock who's value is dependent on a fickle, unpredictable, often cruel market BUT you have a good job in town, a wife with a job, federal disaster insurance or land and farm equipment that can be used as collateral, please press two.

[2] If you have a poultry problem, press one for the Campbells Soup buyer. If you are a pork producer, press two for counseling and hysteria prevention. If your problem concerns cattle, press three.

[3] If the condition is serious enough (over $500) and you can bring the animal to the clinic, press one. If the condition is not life threatening or you do not have a stock trailer, press two.

[2] If you have already been treating this animal yourself for weeks, press one.

[1] If the animal is ambulatory, press one. If the animal is recumbent, press two. If the animal is comatose, press three.

[2] If the animal has been down for less than two days, press one.

[1] If the animal is still eating and drinking, press one. If the animal is not eating but still has a detectable pulse, press two.

[2] We have now reached the critical stage in this automated voice mail Diagnostic Situation Prognosis Assessment Device. Your prognosis is: Poor to partly cloudy - estimated cost $612.00. Add $100 for weekend and after hours - satisfaction barometer – minus 3. If you would like to have the veterinarian make a house call, press one. If you want to kiss it off and bite the bullet, press two for Johansen's Hide and Tallow.

[2] Have a nice day.

DUNNY AND THE DUCK

There are strange tales told in the days of old
When cowboys tested their luck
But the queerest portrayal of life on the trail
Was when Dunny ran off with the duck.

The boys and I were drivin' steers
up north and stopped at Hymer
To rest the bunch and have some lunch
and just restoke our primer.

We tied our horses to the fence,
commenced to tellin' whoppers
And thus inclined, we watched a line
of ducks come huntin' hoppers.

Those ducks fell in behind our steeds
and sorted through their droppings
For bits of grass or oats they'd passed
like barnyard fowl out shopping.

Young Orville hefted up a duck
which kinda starts this caper.
Behind unfazed, ol' Dunny raised
his tail to break a vapor.

Why people do the things they do
remains a constant wonder.
Like Orville there, saw tail mid-air
and stuck the duck up under!

To say it took his breath away
would sure describe ol' Dunny
And just as true, I reckon, too,
that duck was breathin' funny!

'Cause underneath ol' Dunny's tail
two wings protruded oddly
And filled the air with flyin' hair
The racket was ungodly.

You talk about a hissy fit!
Both fur and fowl got ruffled.
Above the din the duck chimed in
although his quack was muffled.

Ol' Dunny rared and broke his reins.
The other horses bolted
And ran askew while feathers flew
like Pegasus had molted!

I saw 'em top a distant hill
and headed home in earnest.
Like somewhere back he'd been attacked
by a drunken taxidermist!

Young Orville took his chewin' square
but, we finally all deduced
By Josephine, we'd never seen
one ducked . . . instead of goosed!

And what about the duck, you ask?
Well, he didn't stay for dinner.
So I don't doubt he stuck it out, or in,
and rode on south for winter!

THE TWENTY-DOLLAR ROPE

Tom says it oughta be against the law to sell a rope for $20. It's like buyin' two white mice for yer kid. They're so cute that first day in their little cage. A five-pound bag of Rodent Chow looks like it'll last forever. By the time you're orderin' 20 tons of Rodent Grower Mix in the bulk, it's too late to call the cat!

Roping starts off innocent enough. Get the feel of it. Maybe buy a dummy head for $28.95 to stick in a haybale in the backyard. Then Alan Bach's book for $19.95 and a $5.00 pair of roping gloves. Just a way to kill time, you say.

Without meaning to, you start hangin' around team ropers. Talk centers around roping. It eventually gets around to horses. Your horse has about as much interest in roping as your wife does! Somebody mentions a good rope horse for sale. Maybe you oughta go look. Only $3,500. No more than a family season ski pass.

You start reading the *Rodeo Sports News* and the *Super Looper.* The saddle you've got is serviceable, but if you expect to win, you need one that is built for ropers. You could order a custom built, of course, but that's too expensive and takes too long to get. You compromise and buy one off the rack for $2,400. Not near as much as a golf cart.

The local jackpot arena is only eight miles from home. Really too far to ride a'horseback twice a week, so you scan the want ads: GOOD USED TWO-HORSE TRAILER - $4,000. Needs a little paint, wiring, license and new tires: another $1,700. Not much more than yer oldest kid's college tuition.

You pull yer new horse trailer to the local ropings in yer four-door Cobalt. That lasts about six weeks. A new four-wheel drive dually pickup, repainted to match the trailer; $48,000. No more than a good water skiing boat. Besides, now you can go to some of the ropin's with the toughs. There's a chance to win some good money.

Sunday night, 11 p.m., yer wife looks up from her pillow and dutifully asks, "Well, dear, how was the roping today?" *"Almost got third money. Dang loop slipped off one hock. Anyway, I only lost $45."*

FROG IN THE PHYSIOLOGY LAB

I remember physiology laboratory in veterinary school. This is where they teach you how the body works. First day the graduate student passed out the instruction sheet. Then he issued everybody a frog. I read the instructions, it said, "Put this frog in the middle of the table." I drew a bullseye right in the center of that table, laid that sucker right in the center of it. According to instructions it said, "Tie up the left front leg of this frog." I didn't have any foot rope handy, finally found some duck tape . . . couldn't find any frog tape!

I taped his left front leg right up next to his body, now he is not likin' this a bit! He was thrashing around and kickin' at it, I had to hit him with a shot of Ace to tone him down. He's standin' there lookin' like he's directing traffic and I'm readin' the instructions, "Make a loud noise over the top of this frog." So I go out and rifle the dumpster and come back with a couple of trash can lids. I get over the top of that frog, I bring them lids together, made a big ol' loud noise over the top of his head and he leaped, I whipped out my slide rule and measured . . . he had lept 4 inches. And I made a note of it.

Then it said, "Tie up the other front leg of this frog." So I tape up the other front leg, made him look like Venus de Milo. He is gettin' antsy, I had to get somebody to ear him down. And, according to instructions, I brought them trash lids together over the top of that frog BANG! And he lept! I whipped out my tape and measured and he had lept 3 inches. And I wrote it down.

Next it said, "Tape up the off hind leg of this frog." This sucker is buckin' and kickin' on us now, you can imagine, we had two guys on the flank, one guy on the ear and the other one bitin' him on the end of his nose. We get that off hind leg taped up. He's standin' there lookin' like a little stork. Then I got my trash can lids and brought together BAMMM! And he leaped! I measured and he had lept 2 inches! And I wrote it down.

Then it said, "Tape up the last hind leg of this frog." Well, we're tryin', he's fightin' and carryin' on, we gotta put a twitch on him and finally got the last hind leg taped up...he looked like a little pillow. I get up on top of the table, stand right over the top of that frog, he was mad, frothin' at the mouth, glarin' up at me, got his ears laid back, then I bring them lids over the top of his

146

head, KABOOM! It made a crash that woke up the students in amphibian therapy class! The glassware rattled and the winders shook but that frog did not move an inch! And I wrote it down.

The graduate student ambled over, said, "Ya done pretty good, son. Can you draw any conclusions from this experiment?"

I glanced at my notes. I said, "Certainly. When you tie up all four legs on a frog, he goes deaf!"

CR

TRIGGERNOMETRY

In the spring of my sophmore year in ag school at NMSU I decided I wanted to try for veterinary school. I went to my advisor and he said I would have to take several more courses before I could even apply.

"Like what?" I asked in innocence.

"Two 4 hour semesters of physics, two 4 hour courses of organic chemistry and a 5 hour calculus and trigonometry class."

"I already took organic chemistry," I said.

"This is the 'real' organic chemistry," he explained.

It sounded duable to me. I signed up and the next fall I dove into the schedule headfirst! Little did I know the pool was drained! I had put off the dreaded math course, the chemistry looked vaguely familiar but the physics baffled me. The first day the physics professor rolled a steel ball down a 4x8 sheet of plywood. "That's physics," he said. That's all I remember about physics!

By mid semester I was going to the bottom like a set of car keys. Looking to hedge my bets I went to the Navy Recruiter in town. I explained I was trying to get into vet school but if I didn't, I intended to join up before the Army drafted me.

"Great," he said. "What do you want to do?"

"I wanna fly them jets off the carrier," I boasted.

"Wonderful," he said, "We're lookin' for boys like you!"

147

I took the physical and the OCS tests and passed. He asked if I was ready. "No," I said, "Let me see how I do."

That semester I got a C in chemistry . . . Yeah! A D in physics . . . Yippeee! I lined up on the final semester. I struggled with the heavy load. The math course was a momentous obstacle . . . let me tell you about that! Every weekday morning at 8 o'clock class took place in a huge auditorium with 400 engineering students. I sat in the back where people like me sit. I couldn't see the blackboard and the professor was a Nobel Prize winner from Pakistan and I couldn't understand a word he said!

As a bonus we had a two hour math lab every Saturday morning. It was like getting your prostate examined every weekend!

In March I sent in my application to CSU. I was not optimistic so I went back to check in with the Navy recruiter to see if I was still eligible. He said I had expired. I took the qualifying tests again. He asked if I was ready. I explained I had applied to vet school but my chances were not good. Soon as I got the word, I told him, I was gonna quit school and come in and sign up.

April 1 I received a letter from CSU. I carried it around all day unopened so no one would see me cry. At home that evening I read the letter; "Mister Black, The College of Veterinary Medicine, Colorado State University is pleased to accept you starting next fall, CONTINGENT on passing the remaining courses!"

I was thrilled, surprised, reinvigorated! I started going to class! By the time I took the finals that semester I knew more about organic chemistry, physics, calculus and trigonometry than I would ever know again in my life! The last day I went around to pickup my grades; chemistry . . . another C! Yee Haw! Physics . . . a D! Pulled that baby outta the fire! Then I went to the small class room where the Saturday math lab took place. I pawed my way through all these geniuses with their flat-tops, slide rules and pocket protectors who were looking at the grades posted on the wall. Finally I could see it; Baca, Baker, Balderama, Black . . . F." I had flunked the course.

I glanced over my shoulder when I heard the strains of *Anchors Away*. "Wait," I said, "Maybe there's a clerical error."

I stood in line to talk to the math graduate student who taught the lab and figured the grades.

I don't know if you can picture a math graduate student in the era of the hippies. I knew they didn't pay them well. She wore the same old scuffed sandals every week, and she didn't have time for a lot of personal grooming. She had a child, you could tell by the Gerber stains on her peasant dress.

I was behind a big tall man who was complaining because he had received a B plus! She was explaining to him, "Mr. Balderama, you came into the finals with a 90 average but you got an 89. You can do the numbers."

He stomped off and I stood in front of the woman who held my life in her hands. I dropped to my knees pleading, "I've been accepted to vet school! All I need to do is pass this course." I was distracted by the peace symbol swinging in her cleavage.

She lifted her clipboard, and looked down at me, "Mr. Black you came into the finals with a 54 average . . ." "I know," I said, "I was comin' on strong!" "But," she said, "You flunked the finals."

"I don't know what more I could do. I was here every Saturday morning, regular as an insulin shot, right back there in corner. I could be here another twenty years and never pass this class . . . "

I felt like a pitiful groveler . . . actually, I was a pitiful groveler.

For a moment she must have drifted from her strict mathematical ethos, because she said, "Mister Black I will give you a D minus . . . on one condition."

I said, "Anything!" And I meant it. I imagined myself doing her laundry all summer or chewing old buffalo hides to make her new sandals . . ."

She said, "I'll give you a D minus if you promise to never take calculus or trigonometry again."

I kissed her stickery ankles and she said, "Next."

EPILOGUE: I regret to say I do not remember her name or what became of her but I hope God has treated her well, because she changed my life. In the space of a few seconds she made a decision, against her good judgment, that gave a less-deserving character another chance.

SHOEIN' PIGEYE

"Just count me out," said Wilford as he lay there in the dirt,
A shoein' rasp behind his ear, a hoof print on his shirt.
"I'll handle this," said Freddie, "You jus' git outta the way.
This sorry bag of buzzard bait has met his match today."

The horse weren't much to look at, just the kind a trader'd buy
But you knew that he was trouble when you looked him in the eye.
It was small and mean and glittered, as deep as Jacob's well,
Like lookin' down the smokestack of the furnace room in Hell.

Freddie grabbed a set of nippers and bent to grab a hoof.
When he woke up...his shoein' chaps were danglin' from the roof.
His shirttail hung in tatters and his watch had come unwound.
The nipper's orbit finally peaked. They clattered to the ground.

"Go get a twitch," said Freddie, "I'm about to clean his clock."
He tied a rope around his neck and fished it past the hock
Then pulled back on the sideline to instill a little fear
When Pigeye bit a good-sized chunk from Wilford's offside ear.

Wilford tangled in the sideline and tried to navigate
Whilst draggin' 'round the horse corral like alligator bait.
Freddie tried to stop this trollin' with a loop around the head,
And it might'a worked if Freddie'd only roped the horse instead

But, of course, he caught pore Wilford, who left a funny track . . .
Sorta like an oil slick, when Freddie jerked the slack.
By now the boys were testy and tired of this travail
They figgered they'd be done by noon but they'd not drove a nail.

"Go git the boss's Humvee! We'll winch him to a post."
They got the cayuse necked up tight, and set to work . . . almost
'Cause the halter broke and Pigeye
walked the length of Freddie's back.
They rolled beneath the axle like two lovers in the sack.

Freddie heard the sound of gunfire like a thousand amplifiers,
"I've got the sucker pinned down, Fred, I shot out all the tires!"
It was dark when Wilford stood up and laid his hammer down.
A gross of crooked horseshoe nails lay scattered all around.

The place looked like a cross between the tomb of Gen'ral Grant
And a Puppy Chow explosion at the Alpo Dog Food plant!

Wilford couldn't move his elbow
but he grinned and proudly said,
"Ol' pard, we done a good day's work," to what was left of Fred.
Freddie crawled out from the wreckage
and staggered to one knee,
"What say we wait till mornin', to put on the other three . . . ?"

Illustration: Charlie Marsh

151

FIVE FLAT

Now everyone I ever knew that did much work with stock
Has spent some time in practice throwin' houlihans at rocks
And be they real cowboys or pretenders with a hat
All dream of ropin' just one steer in five point nothin' flat

Now me, I'm not much differ'nt, I do a little dreamin'
And my dream is usually pleasant but I always wake up screamin'
It's a nightmare rank and scary and it turns me gravy pale
But since y'all are waitin' I'll continue with the tale.

I've made the National Finals down in Vegas, yes, sir ree!
And Leo Camarillo is my heeler, lucky me.
We're almost in the money when we get our final steer
And in my dream I always get to sweatin' right in here.

I'm backed up in the box as the whole crowd quiets down
I shoot a look at Leo and he nods, "Let's go to town!"
My horse is at the ready and the steer is pointed right
We need a 5 point 7 to be champions tonight.

I nod my head and out he comes, a'runnin' straight and true.
I hear the headgate clangin' and we're just a step or two
Behind the poundin' footsteps of that corriente ox.
I see my chance and throw it, not ten feet from the box.

Leo's like a vision of a 'willer' in the wind.
His smooth and graceful loop is flyin' under, down and in.
I look back past my shoulder, see him goin' to the horn
Then I feel that solid jerkin'; fer this moment I was born!

I spin around and face him; check the heels, he's got two!
I hear the flag a 'snappin' and the crowd has come unglued!
I glance up to the scoreboard as the speaker says, "FIVE FLAT!"
I can almost taste that buckle and I'm grinnin' like a cat.

But the crowd begins to groanin'. I get prickles on my skin.
The judge is flaggin' NO TIME and the panic's settin' in!
I look down at the critter, say a prayer but it's too late.
There my head loop, once so pretty, is now a figure eight!

Now Leo don't seem bothered, disappointment, he's above.
But, dang! I'm really hurtin' as I look down at my glove.
It's not humiliation or the fact that I look dumb
I usually wake up screamin' 'cause I've dallied up my thumb!

POO BAH

I BELIEVE HE SAW ME COMIN', HORSE TRADERS USUALLY DO!
"I've got this chestnut gelding, might be just the horse for you.
Two trainers from Kentucky plan to look at him today.
I really shouldn't show him, but first come, first serve, I say.

He's the best I've got to offer, none better anywhere,"
THEN HE SAW ME EYE THE FILLY.
"Except, of course, that mare.
She's raced a million dirt tracks, everyone where I'm not barred."

I RAISED A CROOKED EYEBROW.
"Though, I never ran her hard.
She's as sound as Rockerfeller. As healthy as ol' Shep,"
I FELT THE SCARS WHERE SHE'D BEEN NERVED.
"Precautionary step."

I RAN MY FINGERS DOWN HER LEG.
HER HOCKS WERE BIG AND SOFT.
"Mosquito bites, I reckon. I'll throw in a can of Off."
SHE COUGHED AND RAISED A HEAVE LINE
THAT WOULD SCARE AN AUCTIONEER.
"The pollen count's been high this week, hay fever's bad this year.

I've priced her at a thousand bucks. A bargain any day
But I'd consider half that much, if you took her today."
AS I STARTED FOR THE PICKUP HE PLAYED HIS FINAL ACE.
"She's bred to Poo Bah's brother's son, the finest stud to race."

I HELD MY NOSE TO SHOW HIM
POO BAH WASN'T DIDDLY SQUAT.
HE BLINKED AND QUICKLY ADDED,
"But I don't believe she caught!"

153

HEADER AND HEELER

Some say you can tell the difference between a header and a heeler when they're just standing there. I did a survey with the PRC-XWA, Pro Rodeo Cowboys Ex-Wives Assn, and the Team Roper's Anonymous Halfway House and have come up with the following observations:

A header usually has his hair styled, rather than cut.
A heeler cuts his own hair and always needs a shave!

The header drives a fairly new pickup and trailer with a coordinated paint job.
The heeler's still buyin' recaps and the paint job on his trailer matches the primer on his brother-in-law's barbecue grill!

The header has two horses; his favorite and one in training.
The heeler has one horse, in training . . . and for sale!

The header will discuss the lineage of his horse; he's out of an Easy Jet Mare and a full cousin to San Pepe.
The heeler will discuss the lineage of his tack. "I used to ride broncs in this saddle . . . an Association Tree. I just bolted this horn on and wrapped it with duck tape. Fred Whitfield give me this halter!"

The header has ulcers.
The heeler has a hangover!

And when it's all done and they're back behind the chutes discussing why they lost, whining is the verb. The header, bless his good and noble heart, will blame himself or his horse or his rope or his wrap or his dally or his timing or his technique or the wind or the steer or overtraining.
The heeler blames the header.

154

Illustration: Charlie Marsh

SERIOUS ROPIN'

If yer a sorry roper, friend, let me commiserate
And pass along some wisdom that may help to set you straight.

The reason that yer just no good and why you've never won
Is...You've got the false impression that ropin' should be fun!

Don't kid yourself. It's just like golf. We're talkin' sacrifice!
To rope and win consistently you have to pay the price.

Eliminate the little things that busy up yer life,
Those bothersome distractions like house payments and a wife.

Quit yer job! Forsake the kids! Sell everything you own
And buy a dually gooseneck so you'll never be alone.

Then enter every jackpot where the fools'll take yer check
And practice 'til yer ropin' dummy's got a crooked neck!

Survive on beer and road food. Never falter, never fail
'Cause fingers will grow back, ya know, just like a lizard's tail.

Keep ropin' 'til yer spoken word degenerates to grunts
Or simply, *"I'm a heela...but sometimes I wope the fwonts."*

And maybe you might beat the odds but be prepared because
Each dally man will have to face the roper's mentalpause.

Eventually the time will come when nothin' reconciles.
You'll be burnt out from front to back with cavities and piles,

Yer rope won't reach out like it did, yer loop just won't quite fit.
You can't remember if yer can is filled with beer or spit!

There's only one place left to go, so muster yer resources,
Change yer name and get a loan, start trainin' cutting horses!

156

THE LONG WAY HOME

The light shined through the swingin' doors
And spilled itself into the street.
It stubbed its toe on a shadow
And fell at the cowboy's feet

Who was part inebriated.
Well, really...substantially blitzed!
He listed to port and swayed like
His momentum was on the fritz!

He scanned the customer parking
In search of his faithful old bay.
Lo and behold there was his horse
But facin' the basakwards way!

"Great Scott! My equine's been damaged!
Tampered with!" the cowboy said.
Then reached the brilliant conclusion
That somebody'd cut off his head!

He rode ol' bay back to the ranch
Without even takin' a breath
With his finger in the windpipe
To keep him from bleedin' to death!

ODE TO TRIGGER

Hollywood made movies that
portrayed the Code of the West
and Roy Rogers and Trigger
were surely two of the best

They taught a generation the difference
'tween right and wrong
And left us a trail to follow
and did it all with a song

We praise the brilliant producers
and the actors that drew in the crowd
And all the sidekicks and stuntmen
that made real cowboys proud

And I grant they all deserve credit,
for makin' the movies so good
But Hollywood didn't make Trigger,
Trigger made Hollywood!

HAPPY TRAILS
from the Television Series THE ROY ROGERS SHOW

Words and Music by
DALE EVANS

Slow and Tenderly
E♭6

THE ALL RANCH RODEO

"Twas a matchup made in Elko for the cowboys in the know
Called the Rough and Ready Knock Down Finals
All Ranch Rodeo.
Now the Texans entered up a team they thought could never lose
When they bet their reps against the Jordan Valley buckaroos.

You could tell from where they hailed if you put 'em up for bids,
All the buckaroos wore fancy scarves and Amish lookin' lids
While the Texans wore their jackets
for the brush down in the draws
And them twenty dollar roll-yer-own, cheap Guatemalan straws.

It was Blucher versus Leddy, it was leggin's versus chinks
It was rye versus tequila, it was leppies versus dinks,
It was sagebrush versus cactus, it was ear tick versus fly,
It was Poco Bueno versus sloggers raised on alkali.

The Texans took an early lead, at ropin' showed their stuff,
But the buckin' horse fandango
showed the buckaroos were tough.
They branded in a dead heat, but in deference to the crowd
Each side was harshly penalized for cussin' so dang loud.

So the teams were standin' even when the final contest came,
UNTAMED UNGULATE EXTRACTION,
wild cow milkin', by name.
They loosed the beasts together, left their calves to bawl and mill
And the two teams fell upon 'em like hyenas on a kill.

The buckaroo a'horseback threw his 50-footer right.
He dallied just about the time the Texan's rope came tight.
Their trajectories collided in a bawlin', buckin' wreck,
The ropes and cows got tangled and they wound up neck to neck.

In the meantime two big muggers plus two others brave and bold
Attacked the knot of thrashing hide and tried to get ahold
Of somethin', hoof or horn or foot or spur or can of snoose.
Then, by accident some dummy turned the bawlin' calves a'loose!

There was hair and teeth and eyeballs in the picture now and then,
There was moustache lips and swingin' bags,
some thought they saw a hen
Flashin' briefly through the dust cloud. Wild images remain;
A painting done in cow manure, a mating sandhill crane.

To describe the cataclysm would create an overload,
But a photograph was taken and this is what it showed;
At the summit pointed skyward were the Texas mugger's toes,
One arm around a buckaroo, his fingers up his nose,

Who, in turn was mounted sideways splayed acrost a bally black
Who was layin' on a milker, who was smashed flat on his back.
The braymer cow was balanced on her head amidst the jag,
While the Texan fought her baby for possession of the bag.

From the cyclone flew two milkers, bottles high for all to see
Like two winos at a party where the wine and cheese was free.
The buckaroo's hind leg was draggin' like he'd lost the farm.
But he kept his place by clingin' to the Texan's broken arm.

When they fell across the finish line and tumbled in the dirt
The judge declared the buckaroo the winner by a squirt.
Since the race looked pert near even,
the judge said with a shrug,
"The winner is the cowboy with the most milk in his jug!"

"I object!" cried out the Texan, "Our ol' cow just had three tits!"
"That's a handicap," the judge said, "I admit it's sure the pits,
But in fairness to the buckaroo who dallys for his kicks
If you added all his fingers, he could barely count to six!"

☙

MACHO SURGERY

There's a practice in a practice of a vet who works on horses
That embodies the machismo of their kind.
I was taught this ancient practice, the standing horse castration,
Meaning, both he and I were standing at the time.

To cognize the difficulty, the mule-headedness required
To pursue this task of surgery and cunning
One must grasp its deeper meaning. It's often been compared
To changing fan belts while the engine's running

Or standing on a bar stool taking bets from one and all
You can stick your head up through the ceiling fan
And never touch a single blade, or spill a drop of beer
The epitome of every cultured man

As a student I remember Doctor Voss's demonstration
As he strode up to the stallion's heaving flank,
"Hold him tight!" he told the helpers
who were hanging on the head,
"He can hurt ya," this stud was really rank,

He tried to bite the halter guy but only caught his collar
And slung him to the ground with such a force
His underwear turned inside out! "This is the chosen method
To reduce the chance of injuring the horse."

"You will notice," Doc proceeded,
"That I grasp and pull down firmly.
Some resist," (Really? I reckon I would, too!)
With syringe and anesthetic he injected both the cords
Then, finished, backed away a step or two

"Now we wait." "Obviously," said a student in the back
who knew it all,
"To allow the Lidocaine to take effect."
Dr. Voss looked at him blankly.
"No, so you can quit shaking
Long enough to go ahead and testisect!"

Lest you think this macho culture is confined to men alone
I remind you lady vets now rule the world
And a veterinary practice that might specialize in equine
Can easily be run by boy or girl.

And I can personally attest that cutting horses standing
Is a gender neutral practice in vet med.
'Cause last weekend Doctor Nancy examined my old pony
And I saw the ceiling fan scars on her head!

THE VET'INARY'S LAUNDRY

There is nothing more disgusting, more deserving to condemn
Than a basket full of laundry from the local D.V.M.!
See, afterbirth is oil base and needs to soak in hot
Like adiposal tissue but blood, of course, is not.

It requires a frigid bath to make the stain repent
Problem with cold water is it sets the tag cement.
Cat hair slips unnoticed even by the sharpest eyer
Then spreads like dying dandelions in contact with the dryer.

Samples long forgotten in pockets pasted shut
Flavor all the laundry with fermented porcine gut.
Organophosphate fragrance gently lingers in the air
Mixing with the rumen contents on his underwear.

Iodine and methyl blue, fetotomy remains,
Dog shampoo, dehorning paste and suppurating drains,
Abscessed ears and hooves and horns
and poop from who knows what!
All gather in the dirty clothes to spot and clot and rot

And later gets recycled as that ever present scum
That's now part of your Maytag living on ad nauseum.
The vet'inary's laundry can disrupt a married life.
It's enough to make you jealous of a truck mechanic's wife!

But there is no lofty moral just a sense of déjà vu,
A warning now remembered, that should have been a clue,
When your groom gave you his hanky as his darling bride-to-be,
You should have been suspicious
when it smelled like tomcat pee!

So don't let bloody coveralls or body parts of cows
Distract you from the promise spoken in your wedding vows.
If laundry's come between you I'd suggest this little trick,
Soak the spots in gasoline and flick it with your BIC!

162

THE HELL CREEK BAR

In the Hell Creek Bar by the light of a star you'll find yourself where the cowboys are all talkin' 'bout horses they've rode. The buckers they've known, the times they've been thrown and the stories they tell might cut to the bone . . . long as the whiskey flowed.

And amongst this crew who'd forked a few, they could rally on and ballyhoo and make ya buy a round or two just to hear one more. They'd crack a smile like a crocodile then try to put the truth on trial and all the while their lies would pile like beernut bags on the barroom floor.

They were kinda loud for a Hi-Line crowd, Jordan tough – Dakota proud, where drawin' out just ain't allowed and you better back yer claim. They'd might concede Texans succeed but the bulk, they'd say, of the saddle bronc breed comes from the land of the Sioux and the Swede and proudly carries the flame.

And I learned right quick in their balliwick it didn't even count a lick if you were a bareback man. "That's child's play," they'd sneer and say, "The only game there is to play is saddle broncs 'cause that's the way it is in ol' Montan.

To slap yer hide on a bareback snide ain't nothin' but a dishrag ride. A good cowboy just can't abide floppin' around that way. Ridin' broncs is an eagle's wing, a prehistoric reckoning, a panther's pulse about to spring, a buckin' horse ballet,

Like skippin' rocks or tickin' clocks, an army tank with Mustang shocks, a magnum load with the hammer cocked, a moment caught in time. Suspended there, this purist pair with Casey-Necktie savoir-faire, two poets in an easy chair makin' ridin' rhyme.

And I'll make a stand that a good one can ride through a storm in ol' Cheyenne, a champagne glass in the hack rein hand and never spill a drop. 'Cause he's a strain of the old time chain who'd ear'em down, grab a hank of mane then swing aboard the hurricane and fan'im till he stopped."

"So, how 'bout you? You forked a few?" He meant to let me parlez voo and prove for true I'd been there, too, whenever the flank man pulls. I said, "Oh, well, I rode a spell," but more than that I didn't tell this hard core Hell Creek clientele 'cause, hell . . . I used to ride bulls!

A GOOD HORSE

He spent his last year living a horse's dream, being loved by a little girl.

A $400 dental bill at age 25 extended his life. I've owned many horses, he's the only one I've ever buried on my place. His greatest trait was that he had try.

"He was hard and tough and wiry, just the sort that won't say die..." was how Banjo Paterson put it in *The Man From Snowy River.*

He made a good cowman out of my daughter, won her a buckle in the team penning. He never placed in the halter class, always a little overweight, a might short. I took a lot of hoorahin' from the well-mounted boys at the roping arena.

"But still so slight and weedy, one would doubt his power to stay and the old man said, 'that horse will never do...' ibid.

But after runnin' 20 steers he was still bursting out of the box, givin' his all, while the other boys were changin' horses or skippin' turns. And solid? Let me tell ya, even with my horseshoeing skills he stayed sound. Every time I'd buy another horse, and like I said I bought many, he'd become my backup.

"He wasn't my best but he was my ace." McWhorter, Black-draught.

He was 13 when we bought him. He'd done ranch work and become a Little Britches all around. When he was 17 he took my son for his first ride at age 0.

"A kid's horse needs a cool head. And with wise ol' Skeeter between their knees they was safe as if in their own beds." McMahan, Skeeter

At age 22 he moved to the ranch with us and started checkin' cows in the brush and rocks. My nephews and nieces and tenderfoot friends were his students. Never a plug, boss at the bunk, a voracious eater, he finally wore down. Despite the dental work and soft feed, his muscles melted away. But his spirit remained. That's when we found him a little girl. She weighed less than a saddle and block of salt. He stumbled a little at the trot but she looked like a rodeo queen on his back.

" . . . To see a fine lady upon a white horse . . ."
- Ride a Cockhorse Anon

Now he's gone. Died in the night. Just quit breathin'.

"Amigo my friend, so true to the end
Eras buen caballo, amigo my friend."
Buffham and Fleming – Amigo

I said a few words over him. Now I've got to go tell the kids.

RUNNIN' WILD HORSES

The chase, the chase, the race is on
  The mustangs in the lead
    The cowboys hot behind the band
      Like centaurs, blurred with speed
        The horses' necks are ringin' wet
From keepin' up the pace
And tears cut tracks into the dust
Upon the rider's face
The rank ol' mare sniffs out the trail
  While never breakin' stride
    But fast behind the wranglers come
      Relentless, on they ride
        Until the canyon walls close in
          And punch'em through the gap
            Where bottled up, they paw and watch
            The cowboy shut the trap
And that's the way it's been out west
  Since Cortez turned'em loose
    We thinned the dinks and with the herd
    We kept an easy truce
        But someone said they'd all die off
        If cowboys had their way
          So they outlawed runnin' horses
          But who am I to say
'Cause, shoot, I'm gettin' older, boys
  And though I miss the chase
    His time, like mine, has come and gone
    We're both so out of place
        The glamour of our way of life
        Belies our common fate
          I'm livin' off my pension check
          And he's a ward of state
But what a time! When he and I
  Ran hard across the land
    Me breathin' heavy down his neck
    Him wearin' no man's brand
        No papers gave us ownership
        To all the ground we trod
          But it belonged to me and him
          As sure as there's a God

And if I could, I'd wish for him
And for myself, likewise
To finally cross the Great Divide
Away from pryin' eyes
So in the end he has a chance
To die with dignity
His carcass laid to rest out there
Where livin', he ran free
And coyotes chew his moldered bones
A fitting epilogue
Instead of smashed up in a can
For someone's townhouse dog.

Illustration: Don Gill

THE BUCKSKIN MARE
Illustrated by Dave Holl

He was every burnt out cowboy that I'd seen a million times
With dead man penny eyes, like tarnished brass,
That reflected accusations of his critics and his crimes
And drowned them in the bottom of a glass.

"He's a victim," said the barkeep, "of a tragic circumstance.
Down deep inside him, bad luck broke an egg.
Now his longtime compañeros and his sagebrush confidants
All treat him like a man whose got the plague."

He was dang sure death warmed over,
Human dust upon the shelf,
Though Grasmere ain't the center of the earth
He appeared like he'd be lonesome at a party for himself
So low was his opinion of his worth

"Pour me two, and make'm doubles."
Then I slid on down the bar
And rested at the corner of his cage.
I had judged him nearly sixty when I saw him from afar
But eye to eye, I'd overshot his age.

'Cause it wasn't time that changed him,
I could see that now up close,
Pure hell had cut those tracks across his face.
His shaking hand picked up the drink,
Then he gestured grandiose,
"This buys you chapter one of my disgrace.

It was twenty years, September, that I first laid eyes on her,
Not far from where this story's bein' told.
She was pretty, in an awkward way,
Though most would not concur,
A bucksin filly, comin' two years old.

We were runnin' wild horses on the Blackstone range that day.
We found'em on the flats right after dawn.
There was me and Tom and Ziggy,
Plus some guys from Diamond A.
They caught our scent and then the race was on!

We hit'em like a hurricane and we pressed'em to the east
A'crowdin'em against the canyon rim
'Til the fear of God was boilin' in the belly of the beast
And chance of their escape was lookin' dim.

We all held the bunch together
And we matched'em stride for stride.
I took the flank so none of them would stray.
Then I saw that buckskin filly take a trail down the side,
I rode on by and let her get away.

'No big deal,' I told my cronies, as we later reminisced
And celebrated with a glass of beer,
'She would'a made poor chicken feed,
So I'm sorta glad I missed.
I'll get her when we crack'em out next year.'

Shor'enuf, next fall we found'em up on California Crick.
The buckskin mare was still amongst the pack.
I had made a little wager and I aimed to make it stick,
Whoever roped her pocketed the jack.

We lined'em out and built our loops then ignoring protocol,
That mare changed course and never missed a beat!
She took dang near the entire bunch
When she climbed the canyon wall
And left us empty handed at her feet.

In the several years that followed she eluded each attempt
To capture her, in fact, she seemed amused
And her reputation deepened, as no doubt, did her contempt
For us, the bumbling cowboys she abused.

The legend of the buckskin mare, which to me, was overblown,
Was bunkhouse, barroom gossip everywhere.
She achieved a kinda stature,
Way beyond mere flesh and bone,
And stories of her deeds would raise your hair.

Some attributed her prowess to a freak in Nature's Law.
Still others said she was the devil's spawn
So the incident that happened at the top of Sheepshead Draw
Served notice hell's account was overdrawn.

'Cause upon that fateful gather there was one foolhardy dope,
A greenhorn kid who didn't have a care
But susceptible to eggin' and right handy with a rope
So, 'course we pumped him up about the mare.

He was lathered up and tickin' like an ol' two dollar watch
When we spotted the object of the game.
Though we wanted other horses,
Each one ached to carve his notch
On the bucksin mare, Bruneau Canyon's fame.

They were down amongst the willers by a muddy water hole.
The kid went first. He had her in his sights
And halfway up on the other side
Where the slick rock takes its toll
He caught that buckskin legend dead to rights!

He was screamin' bloody murder as she clawed her way uphill!
He pitched the slack and pulled his horse up hard!
She was jerked around and faced the kid,
and friend, if looks could kill
I'd have folded before she played her card.

But the kid began descending
With his back turned toward the mare
He planned to choke her down, I won't deny,
But she jumped from high above him,
Like a bird takes to the air,
She looked for all the world like she could fly.

Time was frozen for an instant as she leaped out into space,
A piece from some unholy carousel
And I stared, slack jawed and helpless,
In the morbid scene's embrace,
Oddly peaceful, until the hammer fell.

She came down like fallin' timber! Like a screamin' mortar shell
And scattered terra firma in her wake!
She lit runnin' off his wrong side like a thoroughbred gazelle!
That nylon rope was hissin' like a snake!

It flipped behind the kid's own horse.
Laid the trip as sweet as pie.
She thundered by him takin' up the slack!
The rope drew tight around his hocks,
Then she shifted into high
And jerked that horse right over on his back!

'Course the kid fell backwards with him.
In my heart I knew his fate.
His soul was headed for the great beyond.
She was draggin' horse and rider like a bundle of deadweight
When Clay rode in and cut the fatal bond.

She escaped. That goes unspoken,
Toward the seeding to the west.
To our dismay the kid had breathed his last.
She had spread his brains all over,
But ol' Maxie said it best,
'That's what ya get fer tyin' hard and fast.'

The years creaked by like achin' joints.
Driftin' cowboys came and went.
The bucksin mare, she held her own and stayed.
She became a constant rumor and engendered discontent
Among the bucks whose reps had not been made.

But to me she was an omen. Like a black cat on the prowl.
I had no admiration for her kind.
She began to stalk my nightmares, an obsession loud and foul
Only drinkin' would get her off my mind.

There were still a few ol' timers
Like Jess and Dale, Chuck and Al,
Who spoke of her as one without a fault.
They bragged her up, which didn't do a thing for my morale
'Cause I'd begun to dread each new assault.

But I went, like I did always, when they organized last year.
We met at Simplot's Sheep Crick winter camp
Then headed east toward J P Point, it was sunny, warm and clear
But I was cold. My bones were feelin' damp.

It was getting close to lunch time when we finally cut their track
And found'em at the Bruneau Canyon's verge.
We rode in like mad Apaches! I was leadin' the attack!
The first to see us comin' was the scourge.

173

The scourge of all my sleepless nights.
The bogeyman in my dreams.
I told myself, this run would be her last.
She ducked across my horse's nose, to draw me out, it seems.
I followed suit and then the die was cast.

She went straight for Bruneau Canyon
Made a B-line for the edge.
My head was ringin'
With her siren's song
Then she hesitated briefly,
Sorta hung there on the ledge
Like she was darin' me
To come along.

Then she wheeled,
without a 'by yer leave'
And disappeared from view.
I reached the precipice
And never slowed!

I could hear the boys shoutin' but by then I think they knew
I was rabid and ready to explode!

We landed like an avalanche, my horse, a livin' landslide!
I'll never know just how he kept his feet.
My boot hooked on a buckbrush limb
And whipped me like a riptide,
And in the crash, I durn near lost my seat!

But I kept the spurs dug in him as I held the mare in sight.
Varmints skittered,
As down the side we tore!
There were boulders
big as boxcars,
Rocks who'd never lost a fight,
That stepped aside
To watch
this private war.

Then the cunning crowbait got me! She came up to this ravine
And jumped it! Looked to me like just for show.
But I reined up hard and halted. There was twenty feet between
My horse's hooves and sure death down below.

But no horse, no fleabag mustang, was a match for my resolve.
I drove the steel in my pony's hide
'Til he leaped above the chasm! I could feel his fear dissolve
As we sailed, soaring, flaunting suicide!

An eternity of seconds that concluded in a wreck
The like of which you've never seen before.
Nearly cleared the far embankment,
Got his front feet on the deck
And pawed like someone swimmin' for the shore!

Then he shook one final shudder
And went limp between my knees.
I scrambled off him, prayin' not to fall.
He'd impaled himself upon a rock and died without a wheeze,
His guts a'stringin' down the crevice wall.

Then his carcass started saggin' slippin' off the bloody skewer.
I lunged to save my rifle from the slide!
My revenge was all that mattered, a disease that had no cure
Save the stretchin' of one ol' buckskin's hide.

175

I stood up and tried to spot her but my head was feelin' light,
I knew she might be hidin' any place.
Then I heard some pebbles clatter up above and to my right
And there she waited . . . laughing in my face.

She was standin' like a statue and was backlit by the sun.
I shook so hard coins rattled in my jeans.
I could feel my heartbeat poundin' like the recoil of a gun.
My rowels were janglin' tunes like tambourines.

As I raised the shakin' rifle, bugs were crawlin' in my veins.
I levered in a shell for her demise.
A thirty-thirty center fire,
One hundred and fifty grains,
And shot'er dead...
Right between the eyes.

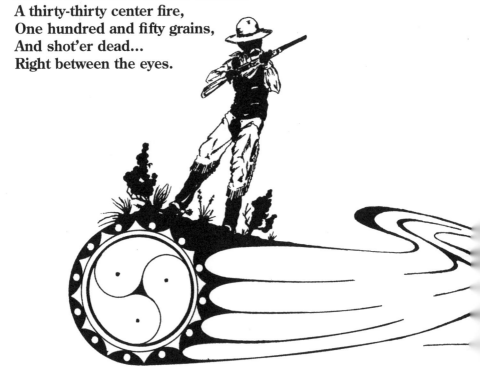

You could hear that gunshot echo all the way to Mountain Home.
The rolling boom just seemed to stay and stay
And it drummed its disapproval like a dying metronome,
A requiem that haunts me to this day.

I climbed out of Bruneau Canyon with my saddle and my gear.
A grizzly greeting filled me with despair.
See, my so-called friends left me to rot.
The reason why, was clear,
They'd staked a cross . . . in honor of the mare.

The rest, well, you can figger out.
But my daddy always said,
'You gotta play the hand that you been dealt.'
I done made that sow a martyr
And I wish that I was dead.
Because, my friend,
I know how Judas felt."

CHAPTER 5
FARMING, THE WEATHER

You will find us on the outskirts coaxing bounty from the ground. With our watchful eyes cast skyward, well beyond the lights of town." - OF THE LAND

When man learned to grow things to eat, rather than to hunt and gather, civilization as we know it, became possible. The importance of farming is not hard to fathom. As someone once said, "If one has enough to eat, he has many problems. If he does not have enough to eat, he has one problem."

In the U.S. today less than 2% of the population is involved in production agriculture. 2% of us are feeding everyone else. This is possible only through the advances in technology in use today in modern agricultural practices.

But in spite of the gravity and responsibility of modern agriculture, the act of farming boils down to one person, down on one knee, at the edge of a field, checking the soil and glancing at the sky. Simply put, it is the farmer's job to turn water and dirt into food.

Farmers hold one of the few truly essential jobs on earth. This does not mean that everything goes right! Just ask a farmer's wife. If he's not broke down in the field, he's broke down somewhere else. That's pretty much the farmer's story.

We who make a living off the land are at the mercy of the weather.

"He'll be back tomorrow if somethin' don't change,
Just hangin' on, hopin', and prayin' for rain." - HANGIN' ON,
HOPIN', AND PRAYIN' FOR RAIN

HANGIN' ON, HOPIN' AND PRAYIN' FOR RAIN

There's a fingernail moon hangin' low in the sky.
The crickets make small talk as he passes by.

As the gentlest breeze stirs what's left of his hair
He spits and sniffs it, but no moisture there.

He stares at the field and remembers the year
These same eighty acres paid the loan free and clear.

But these last thirty days have scared him to death.
The dirt's as dry as a horny toad's breath.

He called up his banker after supper tonight,
They talked for an hour and he's sure gettin' tight.

Ol' Thelma had kissed him
and went on to bed
So he took a walk,
thought it might clear his head.

The doctor has told him
he has to slow down,
Sell out the home place
and move into town.

'Move into town!
What the heck would he do?'
He shook off the thought
and took a fresh chew.

A bachelor cloud,
thin as fog on a mirror,
Crossed over the moon
and then disappeared.

He sniffs at the air
that's still as dry as a bone,
And takes one more look
at the seeds that he's sown.

He'll be back tomorrow
if somethin' don't change,
Just hangin' on, hopin',
and prayin' for rain.

180

Illustration: Bob Black

FEAST OR FAMINE

In feast or famine, at least examine the game we came to play
'Cause win or lose, it's how we use the cards that come our way...

"Just let'er rain," the rancher said, "We've built up quite a thirst.
I know the low road's plum washed out,
the tank dam's bound to burst.
We'll have to plant the wheat again and clean the water gaps
But you won't hear this fool complain if it reaches to my chaps!

The truth is, friends, we've needed this.
We've been so dry so long
I thought I'd have to sell the cows and pay the piper's song.
The winter grass just lay there, stiff, for months it never changed.
I'd walk out through the cracklin' brown
that covered all my range

And watch the wind blow dust clouds
where the good grass shoulda been.
I'd count the bales in the stack and calculate again
The days of feedin' I had left before I'd have to face
The ultimate decision, what I'd do to save the place.

The weatherman was helpful, 'cept he always told the truth!
Piddlin' chance of ten percent meant it just rained in Duluth!
That's nice for Minnesota but it don't help me a bit,
I gave up chewin' Red Man so I wouldn't have to spit!

But he said last night, 'a chance of rain.' More than just a trace.
I washed the car and left the windows open just in case
And sure enough this mornin' big ol' clouds came rollin' in.
They parked above the driveway and the thunder made a din

That rattled all the winders in the house where I sat still.
And at two it started rainin'. I still ain't got my fill.
It's comin' down in buckets like it's payin' back a debt,
Me? I'm standin' in the front yard, in my shorts and soakin' wet!

When the sun comes out tomorrow and sparkles all around
Off pools and puddles standin'
like big diamonds on the ground
I'll remember feast or famine, but when it comes to rain
Ya take the feast when offered, if ya live out on the plain."

181

COFFEE SHOP COMMUNION

You'll find 'em at the sale barn
They've got the front row seat
But they ain't bought a day-old calf
Since Tricker gave up Treat!

They gather at the farm sale
Although they never bid
They'll tell you if you paid too much
And, sure enough...you did!

They cover all the bases,
Like doctors makin' rounds,
To get each gruesome detail right
And then they meet in town.

At coffee shop communion
Where reg'lar clientele
Present their unique points of view
Like it was show and tell.

They sift through all the gossip
Like judges on the bench
And search to find a shred of truth
Among the evidence.

What's happened to the country?
What's wrong with kids today?
Who was the last good President?
How 'bout the price of hay?

They solve the world's problems,
Sacrificing to it,
And if you ask 'em, "Why?", they say,
"Someone's gotta do it."

Lord knows it isn't easy
When mankind's gone awry
But still they toil, pausing just
To take a bite of pie.

They've raised their humble pastime
To greatness, there's no doubt
And they deserve a black belt in
The art of hangin' out.

A shrine should be erected
In every town's café
In honor of the miracles
Performed there without pay.

"Upon this site each week day,"
Would read the simple plaque,
"Six deacons in their seed corn caps
Turn rumors into fact!"

THE CALIFORNIA FARMER

The California farmer is possessed of a mystique
The rest of us sodbusters hold in awe and find unique

The abundance of their harvest, its variety and means
Is impressive to a farmer who grows corn and soybeans.

Now, it's not that we're not farmers in New York or Minnesota
But there ain't a sprig of artichoke in all of North Dakota!

Pistachios in Kansas and kiwis in Montana
Are scarcer than a fig tree in the state of Alabama.

And where did they get kumquats? Is broccoli Japanese?
And why do all their Holstein cows speak Dutch and Portuguese?

But California's bounty isn't all just Providence,
Some credit should be given to its early immigrants.

The California farmer has evolved since he began.
The land of milk and honey drew a simple kind of man.

They arrived with expectations in their worn out cars and boots,
They're amazed at their good fortune, they remember humble roots

'Cause they think that they're still dreamin', not sure it's gonna last
Like a starvin' cow that overnight is belly deep in grass.

So, in spite of their production and hi tech economics,
They're just like us, they mostly read the market and the comics.

Yup, the California farmer, when you turn up all the lights
Ain't nothin' but an Okie with a loan and water rights!

MY KINDA TRUCK

I like a pickup that looks like a truck and not like a tropical fish.
Or a two-ton poodle with running lights
or a mutant frog on a leash.

Give me one tough as a cast iron skillet
With a bumper that's extra large
And a hood that weighs over eighty-five pounds
And looks like the prow on a barge.

I like style but since when should a truck
Be touted for comfort and ride?
Power windows on pickups? Reminds me of jeans
With a zipper that zips up the side.

They should soak up the dents of everyday life
Like a boxer losin' his teeth.
And I like a truck, when you lift up the hood
You can see the ground underneath!

Pickups are kinda like welding gloves.
The pock marks are part of the deal.
Not pretty, just built to get the job done
Like the dummy behind the wheel.

Don't get me wrong, I know beauty's skin deep
and ugly is in the eye,
But to find out if your truck is my kinda truck
here's a test that you can apply:

If you have a small wreck in the parking lot
By backin' a little too far,
Your only worry is how big a mess
You made of the other guy's car!

185

THE CAR WASH

My pickup's no different than the average farm truck. The driver's side cushion is wore through, one window roller is a Vise Grip. The jockey box is full of blinker lights, Phillips screws, electrical connections, needles, old syringes, valuable papers and extra keys to who knows what! Under the seat is a chain, a tree saw, a bird's nest, an official issue tire iron (unused), ant poison, a lumber store red flag and a University of Wyoming archaeological dig.

I never wash it. Lane learned that lesson the hard way. He pulled into the automatic car wash. Loretta took the dog and waited while Lane rode it through.

He sat there enjoyin' a moment's peace and marveled at the modern technology. He watched the soaper, then the big whirling brushes spin up the hood, climb the windshield and crawl over the cab. He remarked to himself how powerfully efficient, safe and virtually foolproof the machinery was. 'Amazing,' he smiled to himself. That was about the time the whirling dervish dropped into the bed of his pickup!

It sounded like a chain saw rippin' through a fifty-five gallon drum! Buckets, paint cans and an airplane wheel sailed out into the street like depth charges! Horseshoes, old bolts, pieces of a disassembled lawn mower carburetor, nails and a socket set filled the air like machine gun fire!

The big brush squealed in pain as a steel fence post went through the observation window! The unit shorted out before the attendant called 911!

Lane spent 45 minutes peelin' 600 rods of baler twine, 12 feet of hog wire, a log chain, two halters and a 35 foot nylon rope out of the big blue brush. By the time he got to sweepin' up, most of the Co-op dog food had dissolved and he could hose it out with the leaves and half a bale of alfalfa.

Now, when he goes to the car wash he leaves his dog in the back of the pickup. Sort of an early warning device.

186

WHY DO THE TREES ALL LEAN IN WYOMING?

He said, "The wind never blows in Wyoming."
I said, "Mister, where you from?
It'll take the top offa big R.C.
Or peel an unripened plum!

Wherever you been, you been lied to!
I lived in Wyoming, I know.
I once seen a horse turned clean inside out
From standin' outside in a blow!

You don't have to shave in the winter.
Just pick a cool, windy place.
Stand there a minute, yer whiskers'll freeze
and break off next to yer face!

They claim that a boxcar in Rawlins,
A Denver and ol' Rio Grande,
Was picked off the track and blowed to the east
And beat the whole train to Cheyenne.

Why, they tell of a feller in Lander
Who jumped off a bale of hay
Before he hit ground the wind picked'im up
He came down in Casper next day!

They don't have to shear sheep in Worland
When they're ready, they wait for a breeze
And bunch'em in draws where the willers are thick
Then pick the wool offa the trees!

But the windiest tale that I heard
Was about the small town of Sinclair.
It used to set on the Idaho line
Then one spring it just blew over there!

I carry this rock in my pocket
For good luck and here's one for you.
Every little bit helps in Wyoming.
If yer skinny you better take two!

Well, stranger, you might just be part right.
Though, fer sure you ain't seen Devil's Tower.
Let's say the wind never blows in Wyoming...
Under eighty-five miles an hour!

187

JANUARY, FEBRUARY, MUD

March comes in like a lion and goes out like a flatbed full of wet carpet. The most I can say about March is, it is a month of change. If March were a person, it would be an old man; cracked and weathered and cantankerous. Occasionally bearable but bent on maintaining his reputation for orneriness. The kind that won't turn up his hearing aid or zip his fly.

In the deep south, March is pleasant. Matter of fact, they even look forward to it. But for most of cow country, the deep south might as well be on the back side of the moon! The March rain up north is not a gentle, life giving shower from Heaven to be savored and sniffed. It's more like the angels hosing out their hog confinement shed!

And the gentle breezes that whisper through the Georgia Yellow Pine aren't even a distant relative to the steady, bone-chilling twenty-mile-an-hour wind that whistles across eastern Idaho.

Even the word March is harsh and conjures up a tough, unforgiving image. Not like light and airy April or comfortable, short February. If I was asked to rename March, I would call it Mud. January, February, Mud . . . Mud 7th . . . the Ides of Mud. Doesn't sound much different, does it?

Mud is a busy time of the year: feedlots are full, calvin' has started, and the lambin' crew is getting the jugs ready. Cowboys are still wearin' their winter long johns and five-buckle overshoes. It's too soon to take the mud and snows off the pickup. The days are getting' longer but nobody knows why.

The horses still have their hairy side out. It is usually the last month you can stick a tractor up to the axle. What most people do in March is look forward to April.

"Well, one good thing about this miserable wind is it'll help dry up the mud."

"We'll be able to get into the fields next month."

"The bulk of the calvin' will be over in three or four weeks."

It seems I ought to have somethin' good to say about March. It's good and cold, good and windy, and good and long. Is that good enough?

I only know one cowman who liked March: McQuilken. He said when it was over at least he knew he still wouldn't have the whole winter to go through. He was just glad it didn't come in November.

Illustration: Don Gill

FARMER OR RANCHER?

There is a distinction in the livestock business between ranchers and farmers. But how does a city slicker tell the difference? I have some guidelines that should be helpful.

1. Ranchers live in the west. Except beet growers in Idaho, cotton farmers in Arizona, prune pickers in California and wheat producers in Montana. Farmers live east of Burlington, Colorado. Except for cattle ranchers in the Sandhills of Nebraska, cracker cowboys in Florida, Flinthills cowmen in Kansas, and mink ranchers in Michigan.

2. Farmers wear seed company caps except when they're attending the Co-Op banquet, the annual cattlemen's meeting or going on a tour to a foreign country. Ranchers wear western hats except when they're team roping, putting up hay or feeding cows at 30° below zero.

3. Ranchers wear western boots except when they're irrigating and sleeping. Farmers wear western boots except when they go to town.

4. Farmers work cows afoot, on a tractor, a four-wheeler, a motorcycle, in the pickup, snowmobile, road grader, canoe or ultralight. Virtually any motorized contraption except a horse. Ranchers work cows horseback.

5. Farmers can identify grass. Ranchers have trouble distinguishing grass from weeds and indoor-outdoor carpet. Farmers think grass is green. Ranchers think it is yellow.

6. Ranchers haul their dogs around in the pickup and pretend they are stock dogs. Farmers usually leave their pets at home.

7. Farmers think a rope is good for towing farm equipment, tying down bales and staking the milk cow along the highway. A rancher's rope hangs on the saddle and is only used to throw at critters.

8. A rancher wouldn't be caught dead in overalls. A farmer never wears a scarf or spurs.

9. Farmers complain about the weather, the market, the government, the banker, taxes, county roads, the price of seed, equipment, veterinary work, pickups, tires and kids. So do ranchers.

Now that I've made it perfectly clear, let's assume you see a man on Main Street in Enid, Oklahoma. He's wearing western boots, a seed corn cap and has a pocketful of pencils. He's driving his pickup complete with a dog, a saddle and a four-wheeler in the back. Which is he, a farmer or a rancher?

He's either a rancher on his way to a roping or a farmer coming back from the flea market. The only way to be sure is to examine his rope. If it has more than two knots in it, he's a farmer!

Illustration: Don Gill

RANGE FIRE

Lightning cracked across the sky
like veins on the back of your hand.
It reached a fiery finger out as if in reprimand
And torched a crippled cottonwood that leaned against the sky
While grass and sagebrush hunkered down that hellish hot July.

The cottonwood exploded! And shot its flaming seeds
Like comets into kerosene, igniting all the weeds.
The air was thick as dog's breath
when the fire's feet hit the ground.
It licked its pyrogenic lips and then it looked around.

The prairie lay defenseless in the pathway of the beast.
It seemed to search the further hills and pointed to the east,
Then charged! Like some blind arsonist,
some heathen hell on wheels
With its felonious companion, the wind, hot on his heels.

The varmints ran like lemmings in the shadow of the flame
While high above a red tailed hawk flew circles, taking aim.
He spied a frazzled prairie dog and banked into a dive
But the stoker saw him comin' and fried 'em both alive!

It slid across the surface like a molten oil slick.
It ran down prey and predator . . . the quiet and the quick.
The killdeer couldn't trick it, it was cinders in a flash.
The bones of all who faced it soon lay smoking in the ash.

The antelope and cricket, the rattlesnake and bee,
The butterfly and badger, the coyote and the flea.
It was faster than the rabbit, faster than the fawn,
They danced inside the dragon's mouth like puppets . . .
then were gone.

It offered up no quarter and burned for seven days.
A hundred thousand acres were consumed within the blaze.
Brave men came out to kill it, cutting trail after trail
But it jumped their puny firebreaks and scattered 'em like quail.

It was ugly from a distance and uglier up close
So said the men who saw the greasy belly of the ghost.
It made'm cry for mama. Blistered paint on D-8 Cats.
It sucked the sweat right off of their backs
and broke their thermostats.

It was hotter than a burning brake, heavy as a train,
It was louder than the nightmare screams of Abel's brother, Cain.

It was war with nature's fury unleashed upon the land
Uncontrollable, enormous, it held the upper hand.

The men retrenched repeatedly, continuously bested
Then finally on the seventh day, like Genesis, it rested.
The black-faced fire fighters stared, unable to believe.
They watched the little wisps of smoke, mistrusting their reprieve.

They knew they hadn't beaten it. They knew beyond a doubt.
Though *News Break* told it different, they knew it just went out.
Must've tired of devastation, grew jaded to the fame.
Simply bored to death of holocaust and walked out of the game.

You can tell yourself . . . *that's crazy.* Fire's not a living thing.
It's only chance combustion, there's no malice in the sting.
You can go to sleep unworried, knowing man is in control,
That these little freaks of nature have no evil in their soul.

But rest assured it's out there and the powder's always primed
And it will be back, you know it . . . it's only biding time
'Til the range turns into kindling and the grass turns into thatch
And a fallen angel tosses out a solitary match.

Illustration: Don Gill

193

RALPH'S TREE

Ralph planted the tree next to the house so it would get run-off from the roof. He put it outside the bathroom window so he and Mary could see it often. As the years slid by Ralph gave it special care. It was strange to see a grizzled old rancher fondly tending his tree. But it grew, which was no small accomplishment in the sun baked prairie of eastern Montana. It withstood the blizzards and dry spells, the searing wind and meager soil, just like the people who inhabit that hard country.

The tree didn't exactly flourish but it lived and grew. It was a symbol. It marked a spot of civilization in an unforgiving land. Ralph rested easier knowing the tree grew in his yard. It gave Mary comfort.

Birds came and nested in it. It stood as tall as it could and did its best to repay Ralph's attention by shading a little more of the house every year. Although Ralph would probably never say it, I figger he loved that tree.

I can understand. I've spent my life planting trees. Wherever I've lived trees were not plentiful . . . the Panhandle of Texas, southern New Mexico, the California desert, the sagebrush country of Idaho, the plains of Colorado and the Arizona borderline. I'd move into a place and plant a few trees. I had to lay pretty flat to get any shade. Then I'd move on before I could hang a hammock. Yup, I know how Ralph felt abut his tree.

The Empire Builder, Amtrak's Pride of the North, runs from Chicago to Spokane. It comes through Ralph's country. Eastern Montana was dry as a Death Valley dirt road that summer of '88. Sparks from the train started a range fire. The wall of flame was 30 feet high and moving 40 mph when Ralph smelled the smoke. He and Mary escaped with their lives and little else. The house, the outbuildings, the machinery and the garden were burned to the ground. They'd been on the ranch 58 years. Fifty-eight years.

They're staying in town now. Their lawyer is working on a settlement with the railroad. It'll take time. Something Ralph doesn't want to waste. He's 81.

Ralph's tree is a stick. As dead as a steel post. As dead as a dream.

Ralph, my heart goes out to you, sir. But I know as sure as the sun comes up tomorrow, you have to plant another tree...and soon.

Then this winter you can look forward to spring when that little tree will leaf out and start casting a shadow on the ashes of your pain.

HELPLESS

"I do solemnly swear, as shepherd of the flock, to accept the responsibility for the animals put in my care. To tend to their basic needs of food and shelter. To minister to their ailments. To put their well being before my own, if need be. And to relieve their pain and suffering up to, and including the final bullet."

"I swear to treat them with respect. To always remember that we have made them dependent on us and therefore have put their lives in our hands."

"As God is my witness."

Helpless.

The worst winter in Dakota's memory, 1997. Cattle losses estimated at 300,000 head. And how did they die? From exposure and lack of feed. Basic needs - food and shelter.

Do you think those Dakota ranchers said, "Well, I'll just close down the store and put on the answering machine. We'll wait 'til the storm blows over. No harm done."

No. They couldn't . . . wouldn't.

"Charles, you can't go out there. The cows are clear over in the west pasture. You can't even see the barn from here."

But he tried anyway. Tried to get the machinery runnin', tried to clear a path, tried to load the hay, tried to find the road.

These are not people who live a pampered life. These are not people who are easily defeated. These are not people who quit trying.

But days and weeks on end of blizzards, blowing snow and fatal wind chills took their toll. Cattle stranded on the open plains with no cover, no protection, no feed, no place to go and no relief from the arctic fury, died in singles and bunches and hundreds and thousands, frozen as hard as iron.

Back in the house sat the rancher and his family, stranded.

195

Unable to do what every fiber in his body willed him to do. Knowing that every hour that he could not tend to his cows, diminished him in some deep, permanent, undefinable way. Changing him forever.

The losses were eventually tallied in number of head and extrapolated to dollars. But dollars were not what kept him pacing the floor at night, looking out the window every two minutes, walking out in it fifty times a day, trying, trying, trying.

Exhaustion, blood shot eyes, caffeine jitters, depression, despair . . . knowing if he only could get to them, he could save them.

Then finally having to face the loss. His failure as a shepherd. That's what kept him trying.

It is hard to comfort a person who has had his spirit battered like that. *"It couldn't be helped." "There was nothing you could do,"* is small consolation. So, all I could say to our fellow stockmen in the Dakotas is, *"In our own way, we understand."*

CR

TAKE YOUR BELONGINGS AND GO

Across the west this summer thousands of people heard the words, "Take your belongings and go." Drought, lightning, careless humans, arsonists and long-standing unnatural conservation policies combined to create a living inferno of our nation's forests and grasslands.

None of which would have mattered much in the grand scheme of things except that man, a recent newcomer to the planet, has begun to amass possessions. They, these 'belongings', distinguish us from the lower beasts. As the billowing thunderous fires inhaled and exploded, threatening houses, cabins, towns and TV towers with immolation, inhabitants in the crosshairs were told to evacuate. Some had a day's warning, some had a few minutes. "Take your belongings," they were told, "and leave."

It is a credit to Homo sapians that the first 'belonging' most evacuees took, after their families were safe, was their pet. Not the entertainment center, the table saw, the sofa, the swamp cooler, the silverware or the $300 Stetson hat. At the top of the list was Sparky or Miss Kitty. Mongrels with no pedigree, bad habits and a $300 vet bill.

And lest we forget, Fury, Dunny and Bossy were led, ridden or hauled out of harm's way before any thought was given to the gun collection, the Frederic Remington print or the trophy saddle in the tack room.

Why do domestic animals rate so high among our possessions? They are surely not more valuable, in dollars and cents. I think we value them differently than inanimate possessions. The word 'love' keeps creeping into the back of my pencil. But love is not quite right. Responsibility is much closer.

It is long standing, this relationship. Genesis says God gave man dominion over the fish, the fowl, the cattle and every creeping thing over all the earth. Dominion is defined as power over, authority, possession, rule and control. God could have said joint custody, equality, visitation rights, mutual exclusivity or time sharing . . . but He didn't.

But dominion implies a reciprocal dependence. It is bone deep in our instinct, caring for the flock. It is deeper than love of the land, the house, the car and even the bass boat.

In the face of this summer's fires, "get the animals out first" seemed to be our first thought. In a world where so much emphasis is placed on material possessions, our relationship with our animals turns out to be one of our most redeeming features.

It makes us almost human.

OF THE LAND

We are of the land. The land that everybody's trying to save.
We are of the earth. Of the earth from the glimmer to the grave.
We're the plankton in the ocean, we're the grass upon the plain,
We're the lichen on the tundra, we're the clevis in the chain.

You will find us on the outskirts
coaxing bounty from the ground
With our watchful eyes cast skyward,
well beyond the lights of town.
Dust to dust we are committed to the earth in which we stand,
We are farmers by our birthright, we're the stewards of the land.

There are those who sit in towers
who pretend to know what's best,
They pontificate and dabble. They bray loudly. They protest
That a peasant can't be trusted with the land to which he's bred
And they rail with the courage of a person who's well-fed.

We have labored through the ages for these power hungry kings.
We have fueled the wars of nations
with their arrows and their slings,
We have fed the teeming masses
with our fish and loaves of bread
So the poor would sit and listen to the words the prophet said.

Mother Earth can be forgiving when, in ignorance, we err.
But, she can die of good intentions.
She needs someone who will care.
Not with platitudes of poets touting blood and sweat and toil,
But with daily care of someone with his hand upon the soil.

Though the bullets become ballots
and the rulers change their names,
They will still march on their bellies,
so our job remains the same.
For the bureaucrats and battleships,
the Einsteins and the choirs
Would spend their life behind the plow, if no one fed their fires.

198

THE BIG HIGH AND LONESOME

The big high and lonesome's a place in my mind
like out from Lakeview to Burns.
Or up on the Judith or at Promontory
'bout where the U P track turns.
It's anywhere you feel tiny when you get a good look at the sky
And sometimes when it's a'stormin'
you can look the Lord in the eye.

I stood and watched in amazement out on San Augustin Plain
While the sky turned as black as the curtains in Hell
and the wind come a'chasin' the rain.
And standing there watching I felt it in the minutes before it arrived
An unearthly stillness prickled my skin
like the storm itself was alive.

When it hit, it hit with a fury. The wind with its sabre unsheathed
led the charge with the scream of a demon;
the storm was barin' its teeth.
The thunder cracked and the sky split apart with a horrible
deafening roar
I felt like a fox in a cage made of bones
in sight of the hounds at the door.

The blackness shook like a she-bear.
The lightening blinded the sun
The rain fell like bullets around me scattering dust like a gun!
It was over as quick as it started leaving it peaceful instead
The only sound was the beat of my heart
pounding inside of my head.

I took off my hat too shaken to move afraid of making a sound
I felt like a man on the head of a pin with nobody else around.
But the sun was already sparkling in raindrops
still wet on my face.
The big high and lonesome is only God's way
of putting a man in his place.

THE AG SURVIVAL TEST

Will you be able to survive in agriculture? Here is a test designed to help you evaluate your chances. Your answers will determine whether you are financially and psychologically fit to continue. Please circle either A) or B).

1. My present financial portfolio includes:
   A) over one million in land and livestock free and clear
   B) a ten year old Ford 3/4 ton, 6 horses worth 32 cents a pound and a wife with a job

2. Most of my ready cash is in:
   A) interest bearing checking accounts
   B) a Copenhagen lid on the bedroom dresser

3. My banker calls me:
   A) "Mister"
   B) every two hours

4. My idea of a sound financial investment is:
   A) undeveloped pasture in downtown Dallas
   B) a racing greyhound

5. My chances of getting a loan are:
   A) sure as the sun rises
   B) as good as Wiley Coyote becoming Pope (Pope Wiley)

6. The best cattle deal I ever made was:
   A) sold 3,000 head of 28 cent Corrientes for 56 cents three months later
   B) stole a truckload of feeder calves and lost $30 a head

7. I started ranching because:
   A) I love the land and inherited $5 million
   B) my daddy chained me to a tractor when I was 6 years old

8. My long term economic plans include:
   A) expansion and increased productivity
   B) winning the jackpot team roping next Friday

9. I intend to ranch and farm as long as I can:
   A) make money
   B) borrow money

10. The reason I ranch and farm today is:
    A) I find it a fascinating and lucrative profession
    B) I'm in too deep to quit

RESULTS: If you circled all A's, you are an optimistic management type with oil on your property. It is highly likely you will survive and invest in satellite technology.

If you circled all B's, you are presently engaged in modern marginal agricultural practices. You will be here tomorrow and the next day, and the next, and the next. Because somebody will always have to be there to do the work.

Illustration: Don Gill

FATHER AND SON

I can't believe he's so ungrateful. I raised him from a pup!
He worked beside me night and day. We never did let up.
He learned to drive a tractor, grease a windmill, pick up rock,
To stack loose hay and irrigate and never watch the clock.

Then after school I'd teach him how to weld and sort the bolts
And to add to his experience, I'd let him ride the colts,
Each summer he spent on the place beneath my watchful eye
Then I sent him off to college thinkin' they would sanctify

All the learnin' I had give him but when he got out, guess what...
He musta slept through classes
'cause he just flat came untaught
He's got all these new ideas about how to run the place.
I've listened to his theories 'til I'm near a basket case!

He's subscribed to every magazine and leaves 'em by my bed
With pages marked for me to read 'bout how the cows are bred,
Or how to increase profits, and to hedge the price we payed.
Heck, he beats me up each mornin' and has the coffee made!

He quotes his old professors who, I'm sure ain't touched a plow.
He forgets that twenty years ago I picked the kind of cow
We should be raisin', but he's so dang enthusiastic!
And my imagination's lost what's left of it's elastic.

I like to think eventually we'll work this whole thing out
And run this place together.
Shoot, that's what farmin's all about.
And we might, if I can just survive these lengthy conversations
And he don't lose his energy before I lose my patience!

RICH FARMING

If wheat gets up to 13 bucks I'll hoard it, yessiree
Till the grain bin's overflowin' or it gets back down to three.
There's too much ridin' on it to sell it right away,
The banker might call in my note they're funny that-a-way.

As long as things are nip and tuck they'll let the balance ride.
Just pay the interest on it and they'll be satisfied.
They don't like sudden changes, conservatives, you see,
They like things they can count on like hail and CRP.

And if you look to go prosperous or friends think that you are
They'll try and sell you somethin' you've lived without, so far.
Like asphalt on the driveway or fancy silverware
Or a double jointed tractor, course, the preacher gets his share

No, there ain't no use me gettin' rich. Knowin' me, I'd spend it.
And borrow more for land and stock.
There's plenty who would lend it.
I'm better off just gettin' by and stayin' where I set
'Cause the more that I make farmin' the more I go in debt.

So, if wheat gets up to 13 I could sell it on the board
But I won't. 'Cause makin' money's one thing I can't afford.
It's a different kind of logic that allows a man to boast
When the richest farmer farmin' is the one that owes the most.

TALK ABOUT THE WEATHER

I've been out on JP Point one spring after the thaw
The water was so thick the fish could walk.
The road was washed out all the way but still I struggled on
Just drove my pickup truck from rock to rock.

And one time up at Grouse Creek it hailed all one day
Then I swear it settled into snow.
We had to dig a tunnel to put cows in the chute
And that's the day I froze off all my toes!

And then down at the Bare Ranch, the fog it was so thick
We didn't need to hold'em in.
We gathered up some 2 by 8's and nailed'em to the air
And hung the gate securely on the end.

At Clipper Flats or Rafter T, I can't remember which
The weather turned off mighty cold indeed.
The wind come blowin' up and got the whip and chill
Right down to minus 99 degrees!

But if you're lookin' fer a hole to send someone you hate
Try the sheep corrals at Cat Creek by the rise.
The only place I ever stood in mud up to my knees
And had the dadgum dust blow in my eyes!

The United States was founded on the premise of religious freedom. Many religions and beliefs exist in our country without predjudice. Christians represent the overwhelming majority thus, they have the most visibility and have the most in common. Christmas is the most popular holiday of the year celebrating the birth of Jesus, followed by Thankgiving which represents the Pilgrims gratitude to God for surviving their first winter. Martin Luther King Day recognizes a Baptist preacher.

CHAPTER 6
CHRISTMAS, HOLIDAYS

Santa Claus and the turkey also figure into the holidays. This allows poets like me to write both respectful stories about Christmas as well as silly ones.

Therein lies the occasional problem, since Rudolph the red-nosed reindeer is not taken from Bible scripture, it is against the law for a poet to use the name without compensating the people who bought the rights from whoever wrote it. Therefore, the name Rudolph is not used in connection to reindeer in this book.

We've not been approached by Frosty, Santa, the Easter Bunny or the Groundhog although I expect we will be receiving a bill from past presidents, should we include them in the observation of President's Day.

Is Piñata a character?

A PARENT'S THOUGHTS AT GRADUATION

Did you ever stop and think to yourself, 'This will be the last time...'

Well, today will be the last time I'll kiss my little girl. Tomorrow she steps into womanhood. Confident, confused, comely, coltish, curious, charming, garrulous, fierce and fearing.

Who will take care of her. Who will she love. What will she remember. What will she forget. What star will guide her.

Will she forgive herself when she can't always live up to her own expectations. Will she choose the right way when the easy path beckons.

Will she discover the difference between pride and vanity, between courage and posing, between distance and privacy.

Will she experience the joy of the golden rule, the heartbreak of losing, the satisfaction of an anonymous kindness, the love of a child.

Will the boulders in her life make her strong or break her spirit.

How will she handle random acts of fate, accidents and blessings. Will she need to assign blame.

Will she make messes or clean them up.

Will she find passion in her life, of the mind and heart. A burning, a yearning, a calling, a cause, a reason to get up every day.

Will she know peace of mind, contentment, solace in her own company.

Will life be good to her.

And will she always know that no matter what happens, I will always love her. That she will carry the burden of my love even when we are separated by miles and years and harsh words and the vacuum of minutiae, even beyond life itself.

So many questions. So, today I stand here, quietly thinking all these thoughts as I watch her whirl about in preoccupied flurry, knowing this will be the last time . . . She will be a woman in the blink of an eye.

And as I kiss her cheek, I can only ask, "Where did she go, this little girl of mine."

A TURKEY'S THOUGHTS AT THANKSGIVING

"I always thought I'd do more with my life. Become a writer, maybe. But it was hard to hold a pencil, I couldn't find a typewriter with the turkey alphabet, it only has 5 letters counting the double B, and it didn't seem right to use a quill.

Like any young polt I entertained the idea of becoming a fireman 'till I found out I was flammable.

As I matured I became active in worthy causes like "Free Tom," and the Turkey Anti-Defamation Society and The 2 Kilometer Turkey Trot to benefit the Dumb Friends League, in which turkeys outnumber cows, the next largest species, by 100 to 1.

I painted signs for the Turkey Illiteracy Foundation. Which was sort of foolish 'cause nobody could read 'em and I couldn't write. I just drew pictures of turkeys looking at pictures. And, of course how could I forget the Anti-Subway Sandwich protest. We held a sit-down strike in front of the local Subway till most of us got run over.

I went through the snood and wattle piercing phase. We thought it looked cool. Then our apartment manager put a band around our ankles. You talk about being decked out. We could rattle when we strutted our stuff.

But it all went by so quickly and now I'm in the prime of life. I look at my contemporaries. We're all grown and have big plans. I've been working on an International Turkey Olympics, maybe hold it in Ankara. With events like Head Bobbing, Track Leaving, Egg Laying for weight and distance.

Lots of people don't give much thought to a turkey's point of view. They just assume we spend all day gobbling at each other, eating bugs and staring into space. In my case I spend most of my time trying to think. Anything, just trying to think anything. When I put my mind on it sometimes I get an idea, as you can tell. The hard part is trying to remember it.

Did I mention politics? I know some may believe there are already too many turkeys in office; but what the heck?

Oh well, people are talking about Thanksgiving. Everybody's goin' home for the holidays. Turkeys are a big part of it, I'm told. I'm not sure exactly what it is we do. But I hope we do it well and that our contribution is appreciated."

HERBERT'S NIGHT OFF

'Twas the night before Christmas and Herbert was lame!
The vet from the North Pole said, "Footrot's to blame
I'll give him some sulfa, it's the best I can do
But stall rest is needed the next week or two."
"Great Scott!" cried old Santy, he turned with a jerk.
"I won't git through Pierre if my headlight don't work!
On Interstate 40 I'll surely get fined
And lost in Wisconsin if I'm flying blind!"

"No cop in his right mind would give any clout
To a geezer who claimed that his reindeer went out!"
He gathered the others, ol' Donner and Blitzen,
Were any among 'em whose nose was transmitzen?
They grunted and strained and sure made a mess
But no noses glowed brightly or ears luminesced.
"It's bad luck in bunches," cried Santy, distressed,
"We'll fly North Pole Airlines, the Red Eye Express!

I'll just check the schedule," he put on his glasses
When up stepped ol' Billy, the goat from Lampasas.
He shivered and shook like a mouse on the Ark
But his horns were a beacon . . . They glowed in the dark!
Santy went crazy! He asked, *"Why?"* with a smile
"I just ate a watch with a radium dial!
Where I come from in Texas we don't have thick hide
My skin is so thin it shines through from inside."

"If that's true then let's feed him!" cried Santy with glee
"Gather everything burnin' and bring it to me!"
So Billy ate flashbulbs and solar collectors,
Electrical eels and road sign reflectors,
Firecracker sparklers, a Lady Schick shaver
And Lifesavers, all of em' wintergreen flavor,
Jelly from phosphorescellous fish,
Day Glow pizza in a glittering dish,

Fireflies and candles and stuff that ignites,
Then had him a big bowl of Northering Lights!
He danced on the rug and petted the cat
And after he'd finished and done all of that
To store up the static 'lectricity better
They forced him to eat two balloons and a sweater!
When he opened his mouth, light fell on the floor

Like the fridge light comes on when you open the door!
His Halloween smile couldn't be better drawn
When he burped accidently, his high beams kicked on!
"Hitch him up!" cried ol' Santy, and they went on their way.
I remember that Christmas to this very day,
The sky was ablaze with the stars shining bright.
They were shooting and falling all through the night.
And I realize now, though my fingers are crossed
What I really was seein' . . . was ol' Billy's exhaust!

Illustration: Bob Black

CHRISTMAS OFFICE PARTY IN THE BARNYARD

At the Christmas office party in the barnyard on the farm,
The domesticated dilberts were dispensing wit and charm.
The fermented grain made scholars out of even dullest fowl,
Though it's hard to take a chicken seriously,
even when she's speaking owl.

Sheep were bunched like secretaries,
sipping wine, comparing notes,
'bout the latest in-house romance and,
like always, blamed the goats.
While the sheep dog and the llama were discussing coyotehood,
and why they liked the N.R.A. and would belong if animals could,
And why it's so misunderstood.

Cows were gathered round the milk bowl with the union Galloway
Who was trying to convince them they should strike for higher hay.
The more they drank the more they
plotted out their smartest moves,
But they finally gave the plan up
'cause it's hard to hold a picket sign,
If all you've got is cloven hooves.

By then the pigs had made a mess of all the hors d'oeuvre trays,
"We're unappreciated swine - You think we live our days
Just eat and drink and wallow but WE have yearnings, too!
We aspire to upper management,
maybe even Vice President in charge of rooting,"
(it was mostly moonshine talkin')
Put a pig in sales now!
It was all this discontentment that had got them feelin' blue.

Farmer Brown announced the bonus like he did most every year.
They could all take Christmas Day off
which was greeted with a cheer.
They had tried to guess the bonus, but like always they could not,
Everytime they were astounded and surprised
which some might think was silly because
it was the same thing every Christmas,
But, like always, they forgot,

As the sun set on the barnyard everybody got depressed,
Just another office party that would fade into the rest.
Till the rooster's inspiration saved this ponderous December,
When he caught the big tom turkey weaving slightly underneath
the mistletoe, mistook him for a piñata and nearly took his
head off with a fence stay, causing a small laceration of the snood
but as memories will attest, made this a Christmas to remember.

Illustration: Bob Black

HOW THE ANGEL GOT ON TOP OF THE CHRISTMAS TREE

This fairy tale answers that age old question, "How did the angel git on top of the Christmas tree?"

Santy wuz settin' there in front of the fireplace, laid out in the Lazy Boy with his feet up. Suddenly he woke up and glanced at his watch. It was 'leven thirty! It wuz Christmas Eve and he had to be outta there by twelve or he wouldn't git all the toys delivered in time!

He jumped up and run to the back room. He tore through the closet lookin' fer his red suit. He shook the moth balls outta the sleeve and slipped into the britches. He heard a great-big-RIP! He backed up to the mirro an' he'd tore the seat right outta them britches. He glanced at his watch and it wuz 25 'til twelve. So he skinned off the britches and run 'em down to the little tailor elves and said, "Boys, sew this back up!" And they did.

Santy come in and throwed on his coat 'n hunted 'round in the closet fer his boots. He couldn't find 'em 'n hollered, "Maw! Where's my boots at?" She said, "They're out on the back porch where you left 'em when ya come in last Christmas!" An' shurnuf, he run out on the back porch they'd built on the single wide 'n there they were. He'd pulled 'em off wet last year and they'd dried out and curled up. He stuffed his feet down in 'em an' dadgum, if the heel didn't fall off the left boot! Santy glanced at his watch. It was 20 'til twelve! He ripped them boots off and took 'em down to the little cobbler elves and said, "Boys, hammer this back on!" And they did.

Santy slipped on his boots and run into the house, grabbed his coat and took out across the yard to hook up the sleigh. The yard light had burnt out and somebody'd left the Fresno parked in the driveway. He hit that sucker at a high lope an' went head over heels and lit with a great big war whoop, spooked the reindeer an' they went over the top rail out into the beet tops! Santy glanced at his watch an' it wuz a quarter 'til twelve!

The little cowboy elves saddled up and brought the reindeer into the barn, put 'em in the hitch and hooked 'em up to the sleigh. Santy jumped up in the buckboard seat, cracked the whip 'n the reindeer took off, an' Santy jis sat there! The tugs had broke on the harness! Santy glanced at his watch. It wuz 10 'til twelve!

Santy said, "Boys, gather up them reindeer and I'll fix the harness." Then he hooked the team back up, leaped in the sleigh and slid on down in front of the house. Just as they pulled up to the house one of the runners fell off the sled! Santy glanced at his watch! It wuz 5 'til twelve! They welded the runner back on and Santy run in the house. He grabbed that big bag o' toys, slung 'em over his shoulder . . . Yup, you guessed it. The bottom tore outta that bag and toys went everywhere!

Santy wuz down on his hands and knees, scrabblin' around stuffin' them toys in a grocery bag when a little angel come flyin' in the door with a Christmas tree over his shoulder. He said, "Santy, where you want me to put this?"

Illustration: Don Gill

213

REINDEER FLU

You remember that Christmas a few years ago
When you waited all night for ol' Santy to show
Well, I heard the reason and it just might be true
The whole bunch came down with the dang reindeer flu!

The cowboy elves had been busy all day
A doctorin' Donner and scatterin' hay
Dancer and Prancer were febrile and snotty
Comet and Cupid went constantly potty

A bad case of shivers made Blitzen get dizzy
He looked like a hairball whose fur had turned frizzy.
Dasher got silly and thought he was Trigger
While Vixen's poor ankles got bigger and bigger

By noon Santy knew they should find substitutes
So the cowboy elves went out searching recruits.
They scoured the Arctic for suitable prey
And brought them together to hook to the sleigh.

When Santy climbed up it was like a bad dream
He stared down the lines at the substitute team
A Bull Moose as old as the planks on the Ark
With a head as big as a hammerhead shark

Stood hitched by a Cow, Mrs. Santy's, of course
Then next in the tugs was a Clydesdale horse
He was paired with an Elk whose antlers were crossed
An Ostrich, a Walrus, an old Albatross

Were harnessed in line but the last volunteer
was a Blue Heeler Dog with only one ear
The cowboy elves gave a push to the sled,
As Santy rared back, cracked his whip, then he said,

"On Cleo, on Leo, on Lefty and Jake,
On Morphus, Redondo, on Lupe and Snake..."
Smoke from the runners cut tracks in the snow
The team headed south, but, where else could they go?

They started back east 'cause it got dark there first
And their luck, which was bad, got progressively worse.

214

By the time they hit Kansas the tugs had gone slack
And all but the Dog were now riding in back.

Santy was desperate. He landed the sleigh
His worn-out recruits were all through for the day.
Bull Moose laid back on the big bag of toys
And jumped when he felt something move...and a noise!

"Let me out! Let me out!" came the boisterous cry
then Jack in the Box sproinged twenty feet high!
Volunteer toys tumbled out on the snow,
"We can help!" said the Frisbee, "Where do we go?"

The Rubber Duck quacked his way to the front
Stepped on a football who let out a punt!
The toys lined up where the Reindeer once flew;
A candy-striped Zebra, a pink Kangaroo,

A basket of Balls; soccer, tennis and base,
A physics professor with pi on his face.
Video games and Ear Buds bombarded,
Uno and Old Maid were young and got carded

T-Rex took his place representing Jurassic
And Obi Wan claimed his Kanobe was classic.
The Crayons got busy all drawing a map
The stuffed Panda Bear wore Trombone for a cap.

Building Blocks spelled Merry Christmas or Bust
While Chemistry's set made the snow luminous.
"We're ready," yelled Scrabble, "Just give us the word!"
So Santy squeezed in by the big DoDo bird.

With a Chrisalling whistle and wink of his eye
The sleigh rose like Dumbo and mounted the sky.
From chimney to chimney, from roof top to lawn
They made their deliveries then right before dawn

They turned toward the North Pole and headed for home
Without Mister Zebra, the Balls or Trombone
The Frisbee was missing, the Rubber Duck, too
The Candy Canes, Crayons and pink Kangaroo

Every tinkling trinket and bundle of joy
Had jumped from the sack, 'cept the very last toy.
The Panda Bear stayed to help Santa Claus steer
Beside the ol' Cow Dog with only one ear.

So if you were the kid who wanted the Panda
For Christmas last year, you're right to demand a
New one, for sure, with his very own Elf
Who can fly, and if need be, deliver himself!

Illustration: Bill Patterson

ALL I WANT FOR CHRISTMAS

All my clothes are laundry
All my socks are fulla holes
I've got t.p. in my hatband
And cardboard in my soles.

I've stuffed the want ad section
Underneath my long-john shirt
And my jacket's held together
By dehornin' blood and dirt.

The leather on my bridle's
Been fixed so many times
My horse looks like that fence post
Where we hang the baler twine.

When I bought that horse he was
As good as most around
But when I sold 'im last month
He brought thirteen cents a pound.

I've been unable lately
To invest in purebred cows
Since my ex-wives and their lawyers
Are dependents of mine, now.

See, my first wife took my saddle
The second skinned my hide
The third one got my deer head
And the last one got my pride.

I've had a run of bad luck
But I think it's gonna peak
'Cause my dog that used to bite me
Got run over just last week.

So all I want for Christmas
Is whatever you can leave
But I'd settle for a new wife
Who would stay through New Year's Eve.

THE LITTLEST SHEPHERD

The night was calm. The sheep were settled in. The dogs hung on the outside ring of the campfire waiting for the three men and boy to finish eating. A coyote howled. Four hundred sixteen ears perked simultaneously, including the 202 sheep. "Better make a circle, boy, before we bed down," said Uncle.

The boy, called Juanito, picked up his long staff, invited a dog and started out in the stubble field. He stopped on the opposite side of the band of sheep. He was scanning their fluffy backs in the moonlight, when he saw a blinding flash and heard a booming soaring crescendo!

He fully expected the sheep to bolt, but they barely stirred. The tumult came from the direction of the sheep camp. He could make out the silhouettes of his two uncles and brother-in-law. Then everything faded to dark. Juanito made his way back around the band to the camp. Sitting on a rough stump by the open fire was a boy his age.

"Don't be scared," said the new boy quietly. "Your kin will be gone for a while but I'll stay and help you with the sheep."

"Who are you?" asked Juanito.
"I'm the angel Floyd."
"No!" said Juanito, disbelieving.

Without seeming to move a muscle, Floyd levitated above Juanito's head. He spread his arms and sang a sweet prolonged note as a bright light glowed from his outstretched hands.

"Chihuahua!" exclaimed Juanito.
"Anything else?" asked Angel Floyd.
"Yes, where did my uncle and them go?"

"To see a baby that will grow up and change the world. Your uncles will become famous because they will be the first to see Him and spread the news. They will be the earth's first Christians.

"They will tell over and over what they saw and heard tonight. They will be revered, sit at emperors' tables, do concerts. They will also be persecuted. The baby will grow and someday will honor them in His teachings. He will call himself a 'shepherd of men'.

218

"Two thousand years from now the world will be singing songs about this very night. Rejoicing and telling stories about the angels and the baby and your uncles and sister's husband. They will be known and loved by mankind forever and forever."

Juanito scratched a stick through the coals. The coyote howled again. He rose to go, paused and asked the angel, "How do I know you're telling the truth?"

"Angels don't lie," said Floyd.

"And," continued Juanito, "How come I didn't get invited to see the baby, and see the world and get famous and all?"

"Well," said the angel, looking him in the eye, "Somebody has to watch the sheep."

Illustration: Charlie Marsh

THE LAST BURRO

He was the last burro left in the dusty corral.

His two companions had been sold by the man. They were younger, stronger and finer looking even by burro standards, which are quite high. They were worth more and brought more money which was what the man needed.

Pickin's were slim. Every evening the man would stake the last burro out down below the spring to graze. During the day he went with the man and packed mud or water or rocks or wood.

One morning the man fed him a small bowl of grain. This continued for several days until the morning the man brushed him down, bobbed his tail and trimmed his long whiskers. Next thing he knew, the burro was blanketed and fit with a pack saddle. Two panyards were hung over the frame and a thick pad was laid between the forks.

The burro watched with his wise burro eyes as the man led the woman out to the hitch rail and gently lifted her up on his pack saddle. The man shouldered his own pack, picked up his walkin' stick and clucked to the burro.

The burro was old but he carried the load as easily as an old man milks a goat. From memory . . . automatic. As he walked down the road he passed his two younger, stronger companions. They were hitched to a water wheel and strained in their harness as they walked round and round. 'Better this than that', thought the last burro.

They walked all day. It was the cool season, his hooves were hard as iron. The woman balanced well.

The second day the woman got off and walked a while. The man tied his pack on the saddle and they walked on. As the days went by the woman got off more often and they'd stop to rest for a while.

They arrived in a town late one night. The man went in a house. The woman waited. Momentarily the man returned and led the burro around back to the stable. The burro was glad to get the saddle off. He was watered, tied in a far corner and fed some grass hay.

The burro watched as the man put a blanket in one of the stalls and laid the woman down. Time passed. Later in the night the woman walked out carrying a man-child and laid him in a hay manger.

The burro slept, as old men do, with one ear cocked. He saw the sheepmen come, he heard the singing. He'd heard it before. The burro had worked the sheep camps.

Next morning the man fed and watered the burro and left. While he was gone the woman picked up the man-child and brought him to the burro. She raised one of his tiny hands and stroked the burro's soft nose. She, herself, patted the burro's neck.

On the trip back home the woman and man-child rode on the burro's back.

As the years went by the woman would bring the growing man-child out to the corral and hold him up or set him on the burro's back. She would talk man-talk to the child. And when the burro got too old to work the man-child would come and stroke his nose and give him a handful of grain.

One day the burro could no longer get up. He became frightened. The woman and the grown young man came to the corral and held his head in their laps. They patted his rough coat and stroked his soft nose. Eventually the burro closed his eyes. He felt a teardrop on his face. It was the last thing he ever felt.

JOE AND MARIA
THE FIRST CHRISTMAS . . . COWBOY STYLE

Now, I 'spect most of you cowboys have heard the story 'bout Christmas. How it came to be an' all, but I wanna 'splain it so y'all kin understand.

It started with this cowboy named Joe. He'd married a girl name Maria. Times was hard in them days. They's down to the crumbly jerky and one ol' paint gelding named Duke. To top it off, Maria was in the family way.

They'd been ridin' several days, with Joe mostly walkin'. They camped on the trail and Maria was gettin' tired an' ornery. Late one night, December 24th, I think, they spotted the lights of a little burg. It was a welcome sight 'cause the weather'd turned coolish.

There was only one hotel in town and Joe offered to chop wood or wash dishes for a room, but they were full up. The clerk said they could lay out their rolls in the livery stable. Git'em outta the wind anyway.

So Joe built 'em a nest in one of the stalls and went out to rustle up some grub. When he came back, Maria was fixin' to have that baby. Well, Joe panicked.

He laid out his slicker, fluffed up the straw and ran down the street lookin' for a doc. By the time he got back Marie'd done had the baby. It was a boy. She had him wiped off and wrapped up in Joe's extra longjohn shirt.

Joe was proud and Maria was already talkin' baby talk to the little one. They discussed what to call him. Joe wouldn't have minded if they'd named him Joe, Jr. but Maria wanted to call him Jesus. A promise she'd made before Joe knew her.

Maria was tuckered. Jesus was sleepin' like a baby and Joe was tickin' like a two dollar watch. Fatherhood had hit him like a bag of loose salt! Just then he heard singin'.

In through the door of the livery come six Mexican sheepherders. They gathered around the baby and said he sure looked good. "Niño especial," they said. Then they laid out some tortillas and commenced to visit.

Suddenly three fellas rode right into the livery. There was two Indian braves and a black cavalry scout. They told Joe that they'd had a vision and followed a star right to this very spot.

Joe said, "No kiddin'?"

"Shore nuf," they said. This was a special baby. He'd be a chief someday. This was good news to Joe. Not only that, they'd brought three buffalo hides, two handmade blankets and a little poke of gold dust which they gave to Joe to use for the baby.

Joe and Maria were overwhelmed. One of the herders tied together a little crib. He packed the bottom with straw and laid a sheepskin over it. Maria laid Baby Jesus in it, and He never woke up; just gurgled and smiled.

Then the whole bunch of 'em stayed up all night talkin' 'bout Christmas.

Joe never forgot. He did his best to raise his son right and when Jesus went on to bigger and better things, Joe'd remember that night. When a handful of strangers helped his little family through a hard time. He told Jesus 'bout it when He was old enough to understand. How just a little kindness to yer fellow man can go a long, long way. Jesus took it to heart.

Illustration: Dave Holl

DAVE HOLL

223

A CHRISTMAS TREE

A Christmas tree is one of those things
Like popcorn balls or angel wings
That children make in the snow.

Things with beauty unsurpassed
That touch our lives but never last
More than a week or so.

It shines from every living room
Like someone in a bright costume
That's happy to see you drop by.

And in a world that never slows down
To see their lights all over town
Warms you up inside.

And it's nice to get to know one well
To know each tinsel and jingle bell
That often as not don't ring.

I can stare at the lights and never stop
Look back at the angel on top
And imagine he can sing.

Even the scraggliest Christmas tree
Seems to have some dignity
Guarding the gifts below.

But all the ones I've seen up close
Seem to be smiling and acting the host
To all who say hello.

Sometimes I think, if I were a tree
The most that I could hope to be
Is one of those wonderful pines.

That gets to spend a week with friends
When even a grown-up kid pretends
That all the world is fine.

FAITH IN CHRISTMAS

It's Christmas time, when we celebrate the birth of Christ. In the U.S., surveys show that more than 80% of us believe in God. That's more people than have lawyers, drive foreign cars, believe DNA is absolute proof, own a home, have been divorced, or watch Oprah!

How can such a high percentage of a highly educated, well-read, technologically and scientifically knowledgeable people believe in an omnipotent being? Where inside of us is the biological process that allows faith to exist? Not just to exist but to flourish. How do you define the words soul, love, compassion, conscience, guilt or sorrow without going outside the parameters of scientific definition?

To choose to believe only what is scientifically provable is to assume, I guess, that all human behavior can be traced to the basic instincts of territoriality, reproduction of species, and survival. That a conscience is a highly refined sophisticated mechanism that somehow helps keep peace in the herd, insures that each member gets her share of the kill, and that each dog in the pack gets a place in the pecking order.

If Earth is truly just a long series of accidental chemical bondings and adaptation to the environment, and God has no hand in it, then those animal rights folks who say a rat is a dog is a baby, are right. Human existence on earth would have no significance, no more than dinosaurs, rocks, oxygen, stars, wars, or renal dialysis. As Bertrand Russell, an atheist, once said, "Unless one assumes a God, any discussion of life's purpose is meaningless."

One of the dilemmas that deep thinkers have, is the need to explain the biological, physical, neural or meteorological mechanisms that allow something to happen. Miracles are hard for them to swallow. There must be some earthly explanation that the Red Sea parted, Lazarus rose from the dead, and Jesus turned water to wine.

It is necessary for them to write off Jesus feeding the multitude. To conclude the Bible is more fiction than fact. That Christmas is just a benign commercial day off.

But for the vast majority of Americans, Christmas is the recognition of something bigger than ourselves. It also strengthens our beliefs and reminds us that Jesus was born to change the world and that He has. Our entire concept of God exists by faith. It's not complicated. When I'm asked if I believe Christ was born of a virgin, I say, of course! If I can believe in something so all mighty, all-powerful and unbelievable as God, I can surely believe Jesus was His son.

Merry Christmas, and God bless you.

CHAPTER 7
ASSORTED
STRAYS

I remember as a young college student taking an English class. We were asked to write a poem.

I was not a poet at the time, but it was an assignment, so I did it. I recall that my poem had religious connotations (Hell was easier to rhyme than Heaven). It was a dark piece of work.

The graded poems were handed back to us by the teacher. At the top right hand corner of my paper was a big red circle drawn with a wax pencil, and in the circle was a big red F! Beneath it he had instructed, "Write about what you know!"

The first 6 chapters of this book are written about what I know.

This final chapter is where I got off the beaten path and let my mind wander. I hope some of them will be useful.

LUTHER AND THE DUCK HUNTIN'

Well, lemme tell ya 'bout my cousin, Luther. Now Luther married Uncle Dink's little girl, Amelda. They lived in Plainview a while, then they moved to Ft. Worth where he's now retired.

Them people down in Oklahoma an' Texas, boy, they are hunters! An' Luther is one jus' like'm. He is a hunter's hunter! Hunt and fish: avid!

He called one winter an' said he wanted to come up and visit an' I said, "Gosh, Luther, be glad to have ya!" Which I wuz.

When they showed up they hadn't been here five minutes when he said he'd shore like to go huntin'. Now, I like hunting, but in moderation. But Luther wanted to go huntin'. He'd heard all about my home state and read our advertizin' in the *Sports And Field*. 'Bout how we had all kinds of birds, big game an' good fishin' and everything else.

I said, "Luther, it's the middle of the winter!"

"Oh," he said, "There's gotta be somethin' open. Call the Fish and Game!"

So I did an' shornuf, it wuz DUCK SEASON!

Now I don't mind tellin' ya, if a guy's gotta nice camper, and a good place to park it an' he can walk from there to the edge of the lake without gettin' his feet wet, ya know, I don't mind huntin'. But I got to tell you, there are some crazy people in the world and the craziest of all them people is duck hunters! Lay out there in the middle of the winter in that freezin' weather in water clear up to their buckle an' then shoot a duck! I jus' never developed a taste for it, I guess.

But Luther had to go! So we went out an' hunted all day on the edge of the lake amongst the cattle. Didn't get duck number one! We come in that night an' I wuz frozen solid! But Luther said, "I tell ya what. There's plenty o' ducks out there, we jus' ain't getting' close enough."

I said, "What are we gonna do?"

He said, "I gotta idea. We'll disguise ourselves as a cow. Then we can sneak right up on 'em."

I said, "Are you crazy! Where are we gonna git a cow disguise!" He said, "Call the packin' house."

So we go down to Armour and picked one up. A big old soggy wet hide with the head still on it. It weighed two hundred pounds! Real fresh. Had big horns.

So there we are the next morning. The sun comin' up over the lake. We're walkin' along the edge of the bank there. Luther's in the front, holdin' up the head and peerin' out through the eye holes. I'm hikin' along there in the back peekin' out . . .

When all of a sudden I see somethin'! I grab Luther by the leg, I say, "Luther! Look around here, boy!"

Luther, he look around an' comin' up behind us wuz a GREAT BIG BULL. I mean that sucker had a smile on his face and he wuz comin' our way!!

I said, "Luther! Whatter we gonna do?"

He said, "I'm gonna start grazin', you better brace yerself!"

Illustration: Don Gill

229

DEEP SEA FISHING

I grew up in Las Cruces, NM and the year I left home the annual rainfall was 3.25 inches.

I swam in irrigation ditches, but the water only came up to my knees, unless you were swept through a culvert, so, suffice it to say, I've never been real comfortable around deep water.

Years later I found myself up in Idaho working for a big livestock operation. We were doing some feed trials for a pharmaceutical company. One day their salesman said that his company wanted to doing something nice for those of us "in the field," so to speak. I told him I could use a new hat, a nice pair of boots, but that was not what they had in mind. They wanted to take a bunch of feedlot cowboys deep sea fishing!

I knew I couldn't turn down this opportunity for the crew so I made the arrangements. We flew from Boise, Idaho to Portland, Oregon, got in a rental unit and drove to Ilwaco, Washington. That is pronounced I L L walko! Upon arrival we went to the first aid station in Ilwaco . . . we were there from happy hour till about 2:30.

The Captain came by at 4 o'clock in the morning! I figger he was a reincarnated dairyman! Who else gets up at 4 am...on purpose! We drove down to the bank and the captain advised that if we were going out on heavy seas, like we're doing today, we should eat ourselves a hearty breakfast. I was from Las Cruces, I didn't know. So I went in and ordered the Fisherman's Special. It was a short stack, a long stack, waffles, biscuits and gravy, juevos rancheros, eggs Benedict, coffee, tea . . . probably what stayed with me the longest, was the homemade corn beef hash.

I have never met anyone who made his own corn beef hash. It comes in a can, like dog food, I know how it comes. But this cook made his own and he was proud of it. Made it with fresh diced bell peppers. Now anybody with a roll of Tums on your person right now, or comes in every evening with that little white ring around your lips from suckin' on that Maalox all day can verify that there are some things that you eat that digest quicker than other things...and fresh diced bell peppers is one of them items comes out the same way it goes in, and it don't make any difference which end it comes out of!

The captain takes us on down to the beach and we board the Leprechaun. And we start out into the bay that dumps out in the ocean and we drive by those fence posts they stick in the water for the seagulls to poop on and I'm feeling a little woozy. So I let myself out on the deck thinking a little fresh air would help . . . and it didn't, so I came back down into the cabin where all my cowboy friends were playin' cards. I sat down and my stomach kept standing up, and the diesel fumes were roaring by my head, and little pieces of bell pepper started working their way up, they hang there in your throat for just a moment then go up and lodge in back of your sinuses where they go off like Sweet Tarts!

I don't know how many of y'all have been eating horse radish and someone made you laugh and you blew it out your nose! It will make your eyes water!

We finally got way out there on the ocean, I knew we were way out there 'cause I looked back to the bank and the people were real tiny! Then they parked that boat, which is a concept I've still never grasped and all my cowboy friends were lined across the back of the boat fishing. I was lined up on the port rail, doubled over . . . CHUMMING, I think they call it.

My friends are sympathetic and they mean well. They come over and hold up this big roast beef sandwich made out of that bread that takes your thumb prints and the Miracle Whip and 3 in One oil are already dripping off the front. They hold it up and say, "Here, eat this. You'll feel better."

" Arrrrrgh, hooooah, ugggghh," I reply racing back to the port rail.

In the middle of the back of this boat is a long white box, about the size of a casket. It is the BAIT BOX. Right beside the bait box is a naugahyde bench, where I am spending the day. And every time the bait boy came over and opened the bait box and drug out big handfuls of fish heads and tuna helper across my body I would get up, go to the rail, "Urhgggggggg, Auawwww, Errrrrrgh."

Finally my friends are getting disgusted with me, and these are not people that are easily disgusted. These are FEEDLOT people. The kind of people who would lance an abscess then take a big dip of Copenhagen and go right on! And these people are getting disgusted with ME! So the next time the big green monster began to rise inside me I refused to humiliate myself anymore in front of my friends. I went over and let myself into a little room that opens on to the deck. A little room they called . . . THE HEAD. It is a nautical term. It is a little room that has a stainless steel bowl . . . with schreech marks on the side . . . blue water with white caps on it!

Are you familiar with the term Tsunami? It is a giant tidal wave that is washing away California.

231

So here I am in the head, heaving in my own private misery when all of a sudden I am afflicted with one of the most malodorous diseases ever to strike a human being . . . yes, friends, I am struck SIMULTANEOUSLY, with the demon . . . calf scours! Oh, NO! So I turn myself in the cramped and crowded HEADquarters, make the proper adjustments and just as I am sighting in, the TSUNAMI strikes the side of the boat!

The sliding door on the head shoots open and fires me out onto the deck where I raced all around the bait box, pants around my ankles, taking little bitty steps till I crashed back into the head where I spent the rest of the day!

I only came away with one tiny bit of wisdom and I'll pass it along to y'all now, if yer ever invited to go deep sea fishing, "Always upchuck to the leeward!"

232

THE HUNTER'S SON

This is the poem of the hunter's son as he tracks the woods alone
And the beaver's revenge when he seeks to avenge
the hunter's gauntlet thrown
By choosing to pair with a grizzly bear, big, nasty and fully grown.

He was raised in the woods and meadow
where ice and forest collide
In the Peace River reach where fathers
still teach their sons how to hunt and provide.

Young Scott was in search of the beaver.
The country was thick with'em then.
Traps were his love but he wasn't
above a rifle shot now and again.

He snuck through the woods like a shadow and stopped
just short of a spring.
There on the bank like a person of rank sat Oscar, the Beaver King.
He was big as a Yellowknife huskie and humming a Rachmaninov,
Scott froze in his track, Oscar never looked back
till he heard the safety click off.
Then he rolled like a log to the water.
The bullet sang just by his ear!
Though caught unaware he escaped by a hair
and Scott saw the King disappear

Scott cursed his bad luck 'cause ol' Oscar
had beaten him just like before
So he turned on the trail, like a dog tuckin' tail
and headed back home sad and sore.

But his path was impeded in progress by a bear
with a griz pedigree.
He was hungry and large, so when he made a charge
Scott climbed up a poplar tree.

He clum till the tree started bendin',
twenty feet up off the ground
He sat in a crotch while the bear carved a notch
each time that he circled around.

He climbed within inches of Scotty
and scared the bee jee outta him,
He snorted and growled and about disemboweled
the poplar tree, root to limb.

But he finally backed off, reconsidered,
like only a grizzly bear could,
He shook a big paw and bid au revoir,
then disappeared into the wood.

Though shaken, Scott felt he had triumphed,
there from his perch in the bleachers.
The vast human brain will always remain
the master of God's lesser creatures.

But the sight he beheld left him chastened,
outwitted by over-achievers.
The bear reappeared, new help commandeered,
with Oscar, the King of the Beavers.

TAKE CARE OF YER FRIENDS

Friend is a word that I don't throw around
Though it's used and abused, I still like the sound.
I save it for people who've done right by me
And I know I can count on if ever need be.

Some of my friends drive big limousines
Own ranches and banks and visit with queens.
And some of my friends are up to their neck
In overdue notes and can't write a check.

They're singers or ropers or writers of prose
And others, God bless 'em, can't blow their own nose!
I guess bein' friends don't have nothin' to do
With talent or money or knowin' who's who.

It's a comf'terbul feelin' when you don't have to care
'Bout choosin' your words or bein' quite fair
'Cause friends'll just listen and let go on by
Those words you don't mean and not bat an eye.

It makes a friend happy to see your success.
They're proud of yer good side and forgive all the rest
And that ain't so easy, all of the time
Sometimes I get crazy and seem to go blind!

Yer friends just might have to take you on home
Or remind you sometime that you're not alone.
Or ever so gently pull you back to the ground
When you think you can fly with no one around.

A hug or a shake, whichever seems right
Is the high point of givin', I'll tellya tonight,
All worldly riches and tributes of men
Can't hold a candle to the worth of a friend.

THE ACCIDENT

My ol' friend Wayne had an accident
Seems he'd treated himself to a nip
And came home late with the bottle stashed
In the pocket there on his right hip.

He fumbled around for the house key
'Cause his wife habitually locked it,
Pushed open the door, slipped on the rug
And the bottle broke in his pocket!

He bit his tongue to stifle a scream!
He could feel the pieces of glass
As they cut through his pants and underwear
Carving X's and O's on his *

He raced to the bathroom to check it
And proceeded to make his repairs,
Depleting the entire first aid kit,
Then he quietly slipped up the stairs.

Next morning he slept like a baby
Til his wife, who was loud as Big Ben,
Shattered his peaceful dreams by saying,
"So, you came home last night ... drunk again!"

"But, Dear, I . . . I thought you were sleeping?"
"Yes, I was, but it's perfectly clear,
I just came up from the downstairs throne
And there's band aids all over the mirror!"

*asterick

Illustration: Bob Black

THE WEST

They don't call it Death Valley for nuthin'
And coyotes don't make a good pet
But livin' out here with the griz and the deer
you pretty much take what you get

And the Rockies have shoulders like granite
They're big and they make their own rules
So take what you need but you better pay heed
'Cause the mountain don't tolerate fools

And the wind is the moan of the prairie
That haunts and bedevils the plains
The soul stealin' kind that can fray a man's mind
Till only his whimper remains

You can stand in the canyon's cathedral
Where water and sky never rest
And know in your bones that the meek, on their own
Will never inherit the West

It's wild and it's wide and it's lonesome
Where the dream of first blood still survives
And it beckons to those who can bid adios
To the comfort of 8 to 5 lives

So come all you brave caballeros
Cinch up and reach down inside
Till you feel the heat, then take a deep seat
'Cause the West, boys, she ain't broke to ride

SO LUCKY TO BE AMERICAN

I am writing this column on my veranda. The heat of the day is dissipating. Shadows are growing longer in the canyon to the south. The bottoms of the clouds are turning pink and the mountains to the east of the valley are glowing purple. Cindy is bustling in the kitchen. I think I smell Teriyaki sauce. My 12-year old is being mauled by 5 little cow dog puppies. The horses are fed. The cows are fat. The quail are chuckling and dusk is waiting in the wings.

As I take a sip of my icy beverage and relax I remind myself of my New Year's resolution; to stop once a day and remind myself that this is as good as it gets. But as that thought sinks in, I become fully aware of how many have given so much so I could be right here. "Right here" for me is to be an American.

Lucky enough to be born in a country where I am free to worship God, free to better myself as best I'm able. Lucky enough to be born in a time when the knowledge of human kind is expanding exponentially, in medicine, physics, transportation, chemistry, extending and improving all our lives.

Lucky to be born while prejudices are fading, poverty is constantly having to be redefined, and America's light continues to shine as a ray of hope for the less fortunate worldwide. But the reality of the debt I owe comes home to roost every day in the papers when I read the names of those soldiers killed in the war on terror.

Every one of them is directly responsible for the freedom I enjoy. They are each one part of a long line of Americans from all walks of life; soldiers, civilians, policemen, firemen, CIA, research scientists, inventors, ministers, teachers, legislators and parents who have sacrificed, toiled, sweated and believed in what America stands for and put their money where their mouth is, whether it's carrying a gun, a stethoscope or flowers to the nursing home.

I owe George Washington, Bill Gates, Grandpa Tommy, Lewis & Clark, Cochise, Federico Peña, Thomas Edison, Uncle Paul, Madeline Albright, Donald Rumsfeld and Pastor Blair.

Two hundred plus years ago a group of citizens as different as Jefferson and Adams or Bush and Gore, conspired to declare our independence and invent a country.

They did just that, like none other on Earth. And that I got so lucky to be blessed to be born here is a miracle I do not take for granted.

I pledge allegiance to the flag of the United States of America.

Illustration: Etienne Etcheverry

240

THE FLAG

Ladies and gentlemen, I give you the flag
That flew over Valley Forge
Was torn in two by the gray and the blue
And bled through two world wars.

I give you the flag that burned in the street
In protest, in anger and shame,
The very same flag that covered the men
Who died defending her name.

We now stand together, Americans all,
Either by choice or by birth
To honor the flag that's flown on the moon
And changed the face of the earth.

History will show this flag stood a friend
To the hungry, the homeless and lost
That a mixture of men as common as clay
Valued one thing beyond cost.

And they've signed it in blood from Bunker Hill
To Saigon, Kuwait, Bosnia
Kabul, Baghdad and Toko Ri.
I give you the flag that says to the world
Each man has a right to be free.

I LIKE OIL

I must confess I like oil and I like factory farming
And I think factory health care is absolutely charming
And factory education lets us school the huddled masses
While Conoco and offshore rigs produce our natural gasses.

Factory transportation is a middle seat in coach
It's soccer moms in minivans, the thrifty man's approach.
If there ain't no fancy Lear jet parked outside your bungalow
It still means you can pack your lunch and stand in line and go!

I love the pharmaceuticals that's given us new life
From cancer cures to botox shots,
reduced our stress and strife
And doubled up our life span, though you hear them cursed a lot
By the very ones whose world they've changed,
I guess they just forgot?

Forgot that all the coal they hate gave birth to industry
That heats our homes and gives us cars and opportunity
And jobs, and time to stop and rest, take respite from the toil.
We built a country, good and great, with blood and sweat and oil.

There's some who smear and denigrate
what they call factory farming
Though we can feed the multitudes, they find it most alarming
"They're using everything," they say, "to make it more efficient.
And cheaper for the common folks.
Do they think that they're omniscient?

Folks, there's nothing wrong with gardens or organic,
we all know
The problem is most can't afford food
that costs so much to grow.

If the world was a perfect place, the 'complaining' crowd's ideal
We'd have no impact on the earth, bananas with no peel,
Forests without clear cut tracts, factories without smoke,
No endless freeways, windmill farms, no global warming jokes.

But none of us, 'specially farmers like the crowding and pollution
But with the help of oil and gas, there came a revolution
Where people could find work to live, and improve their situation
And farmers who could feed themselves,
were asked to feed the nation.

And we who till and mine
and build your malls and schools unending
Leave footprints with each concrete
pour that take millennia in mending
The search to give us all good lives, and all...not just a few,
Should also strive to make our tracks less harmful when we do.

So here we sit on God's green earth, each one a worker bee
Contributing our own small part to have prosperity
And I for one am thankful what oil and factory farming gave
For if we'd stopped each time they whined, we'd still live in a cave!

JUST WORDS

They were just words.

"Tear down this wall!" Reagan to Gorbachev at the Brandenburg Gate, 1987

"Chance of rain." Weatherman in Iowa during the '93 flood.

"Give me liberty or give me death." Patrick Henry, 1775

"I wish I'd never read this book . . . so I could read it again for the first time." Dan Trimble about Hemingway's "Old Man and the Sea." 1992

"The Grass is Always Greener Over the Septic Tank." Erma Bombeck. 1976

We often underestimate the value of words. *"Good job, son." "Best cobbler I ever ate." "Did you paint that yourself?" "I'm really proud of you." "Thank ya, Love."*

We underestimate their power. *"You shouldn't a let that kid beat ya." "Maybe you should lose some weight, Hon." "You should'a tried harder." "Not again, they've heard those stories before." "You do that everytime!"*

There are people whose opinions we truly value. There are people whose praise we'd die for. They are often two different things. Sometimes we genuinely would like to improve ourselves. *"Yer lettin' your rope go too soon." "Give him his head." "Always check the hind feet when you set him up."*

Sometimes we just need encouragement. *"You did the best you could." "You looked like you won from where I sat." "It sure runs better after you worked on it."*

Most everyone is the most important person in someone's life. It is no small responsibility. It should be a crime if we don't realize and recognize that importance because what you say can have such long lasting effect:

"I believe you got the makin's of a world champion." Ty Murray's mom.

244

"I know you can do it, but be careful." James A. Lovell, Jr.'s wife, Apollo 13 crew.

"Believe in yourself." Martin Luther King's Sunday School teacher.

"Ask not what your country can do for you, but what you can do for your country." JFK

"Write about what you know." My college English professor after giving me an F on a poem I wrote for a class assignment.

"You'll never amount to anything." Too many of us, too many times.

Words . . . like burrs under a blanket, like nails in a coffin.

Like a single match in a sea of gasoline.

JUST FRIENDS

I can't remember his number.
I don't call him often enough.
His birthday always escapes me
'cause I don't keep up with that stuff.

And I'm lucky if I see him
even once or twice a year
But I'm really not complainin'
'cause we're still close, we're just not near.

I recognize his daughter's voice.
I remember when she was born.
Shoot, I was there when he got married!
I held the ring his wife has worn

For all these years, his darlin'.
Ya know, she hasn't changed a bit.
And him and me? We're markin' time
by the bad habits that we quit.

Together we're ambidextrous!
Although we're really not a pair
We've got each other covered
and, between us, a full head of hair!

We're part of each other's gristle,
as inveterate as bone.
It's nice how life can fix it
so you don't have to go it alone.

As I sit here blowin' smoke rings
from the pipedreams that I've had,
I'm wonderin' if I've told him
how many times it's made me glad

Just to know he's out there somewhere,
like a dollar in my shoe,
And how much it would please me
if he felt the same way, too.

When I add up all my assets,
he's one thing I can't appraise.
What's a promise or a handshake
or a phone call worth these days?

It's a credit with no limit,
it's a debt that never ends
And I'll owe him 'til forever
'cause you can't be more than friends.

CR

FIRST DANCE

I danced with another woman tonight,
My wife didn't seem to mind.
We took to the floor like a pair of swans
that fate forever entwined.

Leaving our wake through the dancers who flowed
Like notes in search of a song
We tested our two step, tried out a waltz
and laughed when something went wrong!

I led and she followed, trusting each step,
spurred by the beat of the band
Like birds taking wing the very first time,
it helps to hold someone's hand.

Although I had known this woman before
I'd thought of her as a child
But there on the dance floor, arm 'round her waist,
I found my heart was beguiled.

For her a window had opened. I was there,
I'm eternally glad.
The rest of my life I'll remember
the first night
she danced with her dad.

GOOD BYE, OLD MAN

Somewhere deep in the old man's eyes a mem'ry took a'hold.
It fought the ageless undertow that drains and mocks the old.
I wiped a dribble off his chin, "Pop, tell me what you see?"
"It's all the boys I rode with, I think they've come for me."

Unconsciously I checked the door, "It's nothin' but the wind.
You better try and git some rest, tomorrow we'll go in."
*"Is that you, Bob? I can't quite see. Yer mounted mighty well.
You never rode a horse that good when we were raisin' hell."*

"Lie down, old man. There's no one here."
*"No, wait, that looks like Clyde.
He helped me put ol' Blue to sleep. Why, shoot, he even cried.
Now don't forget to check the salt, them cows'll drift back down.
Well, I'll be danged, there's Augustine,
he worked here on the Brown."*

"When I hired on to buckaroo . . . But that's been fifty years."
The old man squinched his rheumy eyes,
I dabbed away the tears.
The boss had told me he was old, had seen a lot of springs.
I bet ya if you peeled his bark, you'd count near eighty rings.

We'd rode the last three summers here together on the rim.
Just he and I, for puncher's pay. I'd learned a lot from him.
But now I'm settin' by his bed, uncertain what to do.
I ain't no good at nursin' coots. I'm only twenty-two.

*"I reckon that I'm ready now. My friends are set to go.
They've got an extra mount cut out that's just for me, I know."*
"You've got to stop this foolish talk! You shouldn't overdo!
Pop, all you need's a good night's sleep. You'll be as good as new."

*"Don't make it complicated, kid, cut a pal some slack.
The saddle on that extra horse...that's my ol' weathered kak.
I'm comin', Bob, I'll be right there,"* He winked a misty eye
And tried to reach up for his hat, then died without a sigh.

I'll tellya, man, it freaked me out! I dang near come in two!
I'd never watched a person die, especially one I knew.
I tried to say a little prayer but all I knew was grace.
So I just said, "Good Bye, Old Man," and covered up his face.

I poured myself the bitter dregs and stood out on the step.
Alone I listened to the night, as still as death, except,
I thought I heard above the coffee sloshin' in my cup
The far off, easy, pleasured sound of old friends catchin' up.

Illustration: Don Gill

I KNOW YOU'LL MISS THIS MAN

The Lord spoke to the heavy hearts that stood with hats in hand
"Your sadness pains me deeply and I know you'll miss this man
But, it's true what you've been hearing,
Heaven is a real place.
That's no small consolation. You should use that fact to face

The emptiness his parting left that seeps into your bones
And draw on it to ease your pain. For he is not alone.
You see, all his friends are up here and all his loved ones, too,
'Cause it wouldn't be a heaven without each one of you.

And heaven for a cowboy is just what you might expect,
It's horses that need tunin' up and heifers that need checked.
It's long rides with a purpose and a code that lights the way
And a satisfying reason to get up every day.

It's the ranch he's always dreamed of and never knew he'd find
And if you think about it, you can see it in your mind.
Him, leanin' in the saddle with his ol' hat on his head,
Contentment set upon his face like blankets on a bed.

The leather creaks a little as he shifts there in the seat.
The bit chains give a jingle when his pony switches feet.
And you somehow get the feelin' that he's sittin' on a throne
A'gazin' out on paradise just like it was his own.

I can promise you he's happy, though I know you can't pretend
You're glad he made the journey. It's too hard to comprehend.
The earthly way you look at things can never satisfy
Your lack of understanding for the answer to the 'Why?'

So, I offer this small comfort to put your grief to rest,
I only take the top hands 'cause my crew's the very best.
And I know it might seem selfish to friends and next of kin
But I needed one more cowboy and Billy fit right in."

JUST A DOG

You were just a dog. But a good dog.

Right from the start. Your loyalty was never in question. And what you didn't know, you didn't know because I never took the time to teach you.

When you were young I was harder on you. I expected you to understand the basics . . . and you learned them. A *"bad dog"* was like a whip on your back.

But when uncontrollable instinct got you in trouble, I didn't hold it against you. I doctored you up, changed your bed and remembered that reason gets left behind in the heat of passion. Be it skunks, gyps or cloven hooves.

You were patient with the young, pups or kids. They pulled your hair, barked around you in circles and rode on your back. I never had to worry. They were safe with you.

You suffered the indignities of veterinary examinations, injections, probings and overnight incarcerations, refusing always to lift your leg under *anyone's* roof.

You posed for pictures, rode on loads like an acrobat and endured spring clippings yet never lost your sense of dignity.

A fierce guardian of your territory, you did your best to protect us. I knew better than to shout you down at two in the morning. I always figgured you were barking for a purpose.

Old age was not unkind to you. Despite the hearing loss, cataracts and stiff joints, you carried on. Sure, I had to help you get in the pickup, but you were part of the crew. I noticed you ate less, slept late and turned gray but you never lost your enthusiasm for bein' part of our outfit.

People debate if dogs have a heaven. I'm not sure that matters. What is heaven to a dog? Enough to eat, something to chase, shade in the summer, someone to scratch your ears and pay you a little attention now and then.

All I know is you added to our life. Companion, listener, guardian, and connection to a part of nature we tend to overlook because we're too busy worrying about the minutia of life.

You reminded us to appreciate a sunny day, a bone to chew and a kind word. You'll be missed around here.

You were just a dog. But you'll be in my heaven. Rest in peace, old friend.

251

DUROC OR CHARDONEY

The pork producers are to be commended. They have worked long and hard to improve the image of pork. For centuries pigs and fat have been connected at the jowl.

Porky, piggish, pig pen, pig-headed. pig-eyed, hoggish, ham handed, hamstrung, pork barrel, hog wash, sow's ear, boar's nest, pig sty and pig in a poke are all terms that have become common when wishing to insult some human's appearance or behavior. I've always admired those resolute loyal women who wore the banner proclaiming them Pork Princess.

But when the farmers changed the product (the market hog himself), they changed the public's perception of pork as well. I thought *The Other White Meat* advertising slogan – a clever tie-in with chicken – was imaginative. I'm amazed how well it has sunk into the consumer's brain. 'Course when they named it that, I don't think the pork producers ever figured it would be the same price!

But be that as it may, I've been plotting their next piggy back advertising relationship. One that will move them into a new level of sophistication and acceptance. How does this sound, "We shall serve no swine before its time."

"That's right friends, National Hog Farms can become the Ernest and Julio Gallo of pork. Imagine two obviously happy, environmentally conscious, grandfather types appearing on the television each holding a smoked ham singing the praises of pork. We'd see billboards with thirty-somethings on a beach somewhere smiling and toasting each other with a cracklin'.

North Carolina would become the Napa Valley of the pig business. People would plan vacations to swine country. They could go by the individual swineries for samples of head cheese, pickled pigs feet, Baco bits, and sausage. On college campuses faculty would engage in swine and cheese parties.

Swine tasting would become an art form. At restaurants the Hamnelier (swine server) would bring out your entrée, cut your first bite using special tongs and a pig sticker (sorry) and proffer it to your lips. You would sniff, suck, masticate, savor and swallow.

"Excellent, Hervé. It has a certain candor, a frankness that says 'I'm from Oklahoma and proud of it.' Haughty, but not coy, a boldness reminiscent of Javelina '13. Yet juicy and succulent, stepping into the new millennium while keeping a cloven appendage firmly ensconced in . . ."

"OH SHUT UP!"

Forgive me, I got carried away. But it's not often I can see this clearly into the future. Pop the Cork on Pork!

VEGETARIAN'S NIGHTMARE

a dissertation on plant's rights

Ladies and diners I make you
A shameful, degrading confession.
A deed of disgrace in the name of good taste
Though I did it, I meant no aggression.

I had planted a garden last April
And lovingly sang it a ballad.
But later in June beneath a full moon
Forgive me, I wanted a salad!

So I slipped out and fondled a carrot
Caressing its feathery top.
With the force of a brute I tore out the root!
It whimpered and came with a pop!

Then laying my hand on a radish
I jerked and it left a small crater.
Then with the blade of my True Value spade
I exhumed a slumbering tater!

Celery I plucked, I twisted a squash!
Tomatoes were wincing in fear.
I choked the Romaine. It screamed out in pain,
Their anguish was filling my ears!
I finally came to the lettuce
As it cringed at the top of the row
With one wicked slice I beheaded it twice
As it writhed, I dealt a death blow.

I butchered the onions and parsley.
My hoe was all covered with gore.
I chopped and I whacked without looking back
Then I stealthily slipped in the door.

My bounty lay naked and dying
So I drowned them to snuff out their life.
I sliced and I peeled as they thrashed and they reeled
On the cutting board under my knife.

I violated tomatoes
So their innards could never survive.
I grated and ground 'til they made not a sound
Then I boiled the tater alive!

Then I took the small broken pieces
I had tortured and killed with my hands
And tossed them together, heedless of whether
They suffered or made their demands.

I ate them. Forgive me, I'm sorry
But hear me, though I'm a beginner
Those plants feel pain, though it's hard to explain
To someone who eats them for dinner!

I intend to begin a crusade for PLANT'S RIGHTS,
including chick peas.
The A.C.L.U. will be helping me too.
In the meantime,
please pass the bleu cheese.

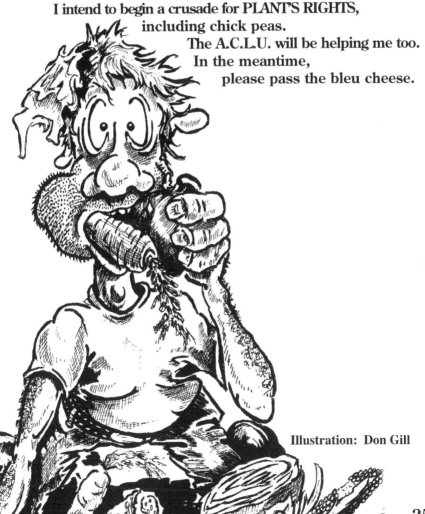

Illustration: Don Gill

THE PERFECT GIFT

For that certain special someone whose talent lays well hidden,
Disguised as *barking spiders,* and often waits unbidden
Until it's least expected then, without a warning flings
It's flatulent crescendo on sulfur scented wings.

What can you give a person with such windy expertise?
A tuning fork? Some Chapstick? A metered time-release?
All ideas with some merit, but may I suggest a pair
Of the latest thing in undies...I call it THUNDERWEAR!

It has acoustic panels to enhance, yet not disturb
The resonant profundo when you activate reverb.
With practice you can dampen those explosive sharp reports
Or by turning up the echo you can yodel through your shorts!

You can imitate a bugling elk, an octopus escape,
Or counterpoint percussion with a Kenny Rogers tape.
Be a foghorn when it's needed, play a tasteful oboe lick
Or recreate an ocean storm complete with Moby . . .

But you say he doesn't need it! He might hurt himself, you fear
But it has its own extinguisher should he flame out while in gear
And to top it off it comes equipped,
            as per the O.S.H.A. warnings,
With protective ankle splash guards for those jalapeño mornings!

And when he wakes and stumbles from your bed at break of dawn
And tunes up like an orchestra awaiting the baton,
He can welcome in the morning with a twenty-gun salute
Or play his reeking bagpipe 'til he's just too pooped to toot!

I know yer thinkin', "I don't know . . .
            a duck call would be cheaper . . ."
But in searching for the perfect gift, one digs a little deeper,
And the icing is this THUNDERWEAR is guaranteed to last
Until his sphincter catches fire or he just runs outta gas!

THE TOAST

It gives me great pleasure to stand here today
To heap limelight on one in our midst
Who has mastered the art of vulgar display
Yet, when asked to desist it...he didst

There are those among us who are more qualified
To encouch in a language precise
The discrepant reasons of why you abide
With us always, like typhus or lice

Why I have been chosen, I cannot explain
I've no keen repartee to impart
But I'm honored, so, though my words may seem plain
Be assured that they come from the heart . . .

You mare ridin', mouth breathin', egg suckin' skunk
Yer the kind who drowns kittens for fun
You hat stealin', hole peepin', pencil neck punk
Yer the blister on everyone's bun

You dog kickin', mule whippin', carp eatin' crud
Yer a bagful of grizzly bear bait
You never sweat, no workin', blank shootin' dud
Yer the reason for bicarbonate

You lackluster, festering, double dumb putz
Yer the wax on a tom turkey's snood
You buzzard breath, bone pickin', big tub of guts
Yer a flake of the first magnitude

You scrofulous, wool slippin', miscreant scum
Yer the grease off a Hell's Angels' comb
You bilgewater, bog drinkin', boot lickin' bum
Yer a bucket of thundermug foam

You counterfeit, card cheatin', commonbred clump
Yer the fungus in old cottage cheese
You back stabbin', beady eyed, Bactrian hump
Yer a throwback to when we climbed trees

To sum up yer good points could be quite a chore
There's so many that it's hard to say
You're either au jus off a dog kennel floor
Or, the nit in a wino's toupee.

Regardless, we love ya. I don't like to boast
But our standards are really quite high
And though you seem lacking, I'll offer a toast
'Cause the truth is, yer our kinda guy!

UNCLE BUCKER'S BABY

I saw Uncle Bucker the other day. He's not really my uncle, that's just what everybody calls him.

"So," I said, "Uncle Bucker, I heard the news. Congratulations! A boy, huh!"

"Yes," he said, "And at my advanced age you can be assured that it wasn't expected!"

"Bucker," says I, "Yer not much over fifty, are ya?"

"Naw, but it was sure a surprise. Miss Mattie suspected something, I guess. She went to the doctor completely unbeknownst to me. When she came back I was standin' there in the livin' room, mindin' my own business.

"She marched in from the garage and stopped, hands on her hips. Close enough that I could see that look. You know the one. It's the same one she uses on the dog when he messes on the carpet. She quickly explained that the rabbit had died. And I didn't even know he was suffering!

"It was such a shock that I lapsed back into my ol' livestock training and began to babble, "Well, yer, uh, bred . . . uh, you'll begin to notice some changes in your body as the gestation progresses, your skin will get smoother and you might . . . bag up a little." "Wait," she says, "Doctor Hamstra told me that no matter what you say, it's not like a cow!"

"So they shamed me into the breathing lessons. Let me tell you, son, you young pups may not realize it but there was a time when expectant fathers engendered respect. There was a special room on the delivery floor for expectant fathers. It had Barcaloungers, ESPN and a wet bar. When the nurse burst in with the good news, you'd stand up and pass out cigars to all your fellow new fathers. You can't even light a cigar in the parking lot at the hospital today!"

"Then you'd rush down the hall, duck in and kiss the new mother and kiss the new baby and go directly...to the bar...where you could be with people who could appreciate your contribution.

You weren't just another face in the delivery room on the second row trying to shoot the video over the crowd.

"So, like I said, they shamed me into the breathing lessons. I think they helped a little. My only real memory of the delivery room was the doctor looking up, from the barrel of the cannon, so to speak, and asking, 'Would you like to cut the cord?'

"I was doubled over a folding chair in the corner, practicing my breathing when Miss Mattie, who had other things on her mind, said, 'No he doesn't!'

"But I'm doin' better now that he's a little older. I was worried for a while. Looked like he was gonna be a farmer."

"Really?" I said.

"Yep. Till he was six months old all he did was milk and scatter manure!"

CR

CAT LAWS

I was reading the paper to the cat last week. She tries to keep up on current events, particularly stories about most-wanted dogs and alien landings. We got to a story where a few obscure animal rights groups were calling for the nation's 66 million pet cats to be kept indoors for life.

"Why?" asked Miss Kitty.

"Well," I answered, "This says that free roaming cats kill from 8 million to 217 million birds a year in Wisconsin alone."

"My, I had no idea there were that many birds in Wisconsin."

"Yes, and one person was quoted as saying 'We don't want our house companions going out and killing other animals.'"

"What about mice?" asked Miss Kitty scratching behind her ear.

"They don't say, but they are also worried about you being eaten by coyotes."

"Then why don't they keep all the coyotes indoors for life? It's like making people bolt and bar their homes and stay inside during prime shopping hours. Why don't they just keep all the criminals indoors for life?"

"Good question, but they say cats are domesticated animals and coyotes are wild animals, and they don't want to appear anti-wildlife."

"Mice are wildlife, so are birds; it's all part of the food chain."

"They apparently want to remove cats from the food chain. For your own protection, of course."

"I thought it was to protect the birds," said Miss Kitty, ever vigilant to flaws in my logic. *"And besides, do they really enjoy that odiferous cat box in the laundry room? It's bad enough to walk around in a Tupperware toilet if you're a cat. I've always envied camels. Sand as far as you can see. Go anytime you please."*

"They suggested that humans who want their cats to spend time outdoors need to invest in an outdoor enclosure or walk their cats on a harness."

Miss Kitty got indignant. *"You ever tried to walk a cat in a harness! We're not dogs, you know! I've spent a lifetime keepin' your place free of rodents and vermin, and this is the thanks I get. So I eat a bird now and then. And another thing, I've lost more friends to car tires than coyotes. Why don't they have speed limits slow enough to let cats get out of the way."*

"Wait a minute," I protested, "It isn't me; it's just a story in the paper."

"Sure," she huffed, *"but some self-appointed cat lover will weasel or badger you into makin' me a house cat. You'll fall for it and take me prisoner. Next thing I know, you'll be takin' me for walks in a cat harness. Not for me, buckaroo, I'm leavin'."*

"Wait," I pleaded, "Where will you go . . ."

"Well," she said, *"I've always wanted to see Wisconsin."*

Illustration: Bob Black

CAJUN DANCE

"Deez gurls ken dance."

He was right. I was flat in the middle of a magic place...Whiskey River Landing on the levee of the Atchafalaya Swamp in "sout Looziana."

The floor was givin' underneath the dancers. The Huval family band was drivin' Cajun music into every crevice and cranny, every pore and fiber, every pop, tinkle and nail hole till the room itself seemed to expand under the pressure.

The slippers glided, stomped, kicked and clacked. They stood on their toes, rocked on their heels, they moved like water skippers on the top of a chocolate swamp. Pausing, sliding, setting, pirouetting, leaping from a starting block, braking to a smooth stop, heaving to, boatlike against a floating pier.

Then off again into the blur of circling bare legs, boot tops, and bon temps all in perfect rhythm to the beating of the bayou heart.

I have lived a fairly long time. I have been places. I have seen bears mate, boats sink, and Gila monsters scurry. I have danced till I couldn't stand up and stood up till I couldn't dance. I've eaten bugs, broccoli and things that crawl on the sea floor. I have seen as far back as Mayan temples, as far away as Betelgeuse and as deep down as Tom Robbins. I have been on *Johnny Carson*, the cover of *USA Today*, and fed the snakes at the Dixie Chicken.

I have held things in my hand that will be here a million years beyond my own existence.

Yet, on that dance floor, I felt a ripple in the universe, a time warp moment when the often unspectacular human race threw its head back and howled at the moon.

Thank you, Napolean; thank you, Canadiens; and thank you, Shirley Cormier and the all-girl Cajun band. It was a crawfish crabmeat carousel, a seafood boudin Creole belle, an Acadian accordian, heavy water gumbo étouffée, Spanish moss jambalaya and a Tabasco popsicle where you suck the head and eat the tail.

My gosh, you can say it again: "Deez gurls ken dance."

I KNOW THAT HAT

I don't know you but I know that hat. I wore a hat just like it.
Back in the days when men were men.
You bet the pot and played to win
And if you lost you tried again. You bet your life I know that hat.

A cowboy gave that hat to me. Back then it was nearly new.
"Wear it well," he said to me, "You're startin' out, the world to see.
I hope you find your destiny," And so I took that cowboy's hat

I put that good ol' hat to work...when work was all I knew
Wrench in hand and on my back, fencing pliers, the ol' line shack,
Horseshoes, ropes and cattle tracks, that hat could hold its own

But then I put my tools away and hung up that ol' hat
I climbed aboard the 'business' train,
faced each mountain as it came
Made my mark and earned a name
and only wore the hat to cool ambition

'Cause I was on the inside rail building cornerstones.
I learned to find my way around, to keep my feet on solid ground,
Not judge a man when he was down.
The hat just took it all in stride...and waited

It watched to see how I would play the cards that I'd been dealt
Would I stay strong through boom or bust?
Would my soul grow or gather dust?
Was I a man someone could trust?
And could I face the man in the mirror.

Nowdays I live my life content, but always thinkin'.
I'm keepin' busy just the same,
Trusting others with the reins, share the praise and take the blame.
It's just the way that life goes when your hand's on the wheel

Yup, I don't know you but I know that hat.
Mine's hanging' on the wall
It just reminds me what it takes to make life good.
Ya get some breaks then give some back for ol' mistakes.
And if you learned life's lessons well, they all can tell.
'Cause if you did, that hat, that good ol' hat...
Still fits your big ol' head.

THE DOG AND THE RABBIT

Have you ever been embarrassed by yer good dog? Me either! I've got a good dog. An Australian shepherd with one blue eye and I believe he loves me. I believe I love him. He'll go with me anywhere. When I say, "You wanna go?" He don't ask, "Where you goin'? Goin' to the video store?" No, he don't care, he just wants to go. And did you ever notice that it don't matter whether you been gone five minutes or five days, yer dog is so glad to see ya. Can you think of a single human that is that glad to see ya. Yer fixin' to leave, walk out to the pickup and forget somethin' so you run back inside. Yer dog licks yer hand. Your spouse says, "I thought you left!"

I've got a neighbor. A good neighbor. And when you live on the outskirts a good neighbor is someone who lives just the right distance away. Close enough to circle the wagons but far enough away to allow that privacy people like us seem to value. *("I believe those are Kansas plates, mother," he said sighting through his binoculars).*

Anyway, she gets home 'bout a quarter after five every day. Goes through the house and comes out the back door wearin' her coveralls. In her backyard she has a long line of rabbit hutches and she spends, what is to me, an inordinate amount of time messin' with them rabbits . . . talkin' to 'em . . . singin' 'em little rabbit songs.

Now I'm sittin' out on the back porch one afternoon in my porch swing. It's about 2:30. I'm done workin'. I've already thought up somethin'. I look out in the driveway and there's my good dog and he has got a . . . and you know how you can tell it ain't a jackrabbit? They aren't black and white, they don't have them big floppy ears, and he has got this rabbit between his teeth and he's thrashin' him like a shark with a ham hock! There's dirt and leaves and brush and gravel flyin' all over. I jumped up and grab that rabbit! "Go git in the pickup you *#@^...!" That rabbit looked bad. Looked like he caught on fire and somebody put him out with the weedeater!

I ran in the house and run the tub full of warm water. Tested it with my elbow. Then I got some of my wife's good shampoo. She gets it at the Holiday Inn, it ain't that big a deal. I sudsed him up twice then moused him with my daughter's mousse. Made him sticky. You could thwack him on the tile, peel him off like Velcro. Then I run upstairs to the laundry and put him in the dryer. When he came out he was fluffy, looked like an electrocuted porcupine!

I carried him to my neighbors house. Sure enuf the last hutch on the end was cocked open and it was empty. I took that rabbit and folded him . . . into a rabbit position. Put a smile on his lips. All three of 'em. Gave him some Copenhagen and leaned him up against the wire.

I went back to the house and commenced to rockin'. 'Bout a quarter after five I saw my neighbor drive up, she got out, went through the house and came out the back wearin' her covies. She started down that long line of rabbit hutches. Talkin' to 'em. Singin' 'em little rabbit songs. "Here comes Peter Cottontail, hoppin' down the bunny trail . . . " All of sudden I heard her scream!

I ran over there, bein' the good neighbor that I was, "What's wrong? What's wrong?"

"My rabbit," she cried.

I looked in the cage and the poor little duffer had fell over. One ear broke off. It didn't look good.

I picked him up, stroked him gently and said, "Ma'am, I b'lieve he is dead."

I was a veterinarian, I could tell that.

"Yes," she said, "But what bothers me is I buried him three days ago!"

Illustration: Charlie Marsh

TRYING TO CLIMB INTO BANJO PATERSON'S BRAIN

I went seeking how he did it. I mean not just how he writ it,
Not in pencil, brush or ink stain or a thumbnail dipped in tar
But just how he played my language,
the proper and the slang which
I myself have twisted into verse and scattered near and far.

Just to spend some time beside him
as the muse roils inside him
Like a seed or yeast or lava that ignites his sharpened quill
I would learn within that hour how the bud becomes a flower
While I watch him take my mother tongue and bend it to his will.

It's the process that I covet, great magicians make us love it
But alas not every oyster can make a grain of sand a pearl,
DNA is overrated, rhyming verse is complicated
And the Banjo ranks in my book as best poet in the world.

It's a bit like building arches with each syllable he marches
Cross the consciousness of listeners who anticipate the ride
And a lilting rises from it, I'm convinced that he must hum it
As he locks in rhyme and meter like the moon conducts the tide.

He's a sculptor carving fiction using consonants and diction
To create poetic mountains moles like me could never climb
I dissect the rhyme and meter,
how it plays through wolf or tweeter
And no matter my attempts I am found wanting every time.

He's the Einstein, the Da Vinci, like them with every inch he
Built a monument to genius, deftly chiseled from thin air
Laying lines of letters lyrical, each uncut gem a miracle
And then welded into meter perfect as an answered prayer.

When you're good at some endeavor
and you work hell bent for leather
You eventually get very good, of which you can be proud
But – if you're naturally gifted like the man who never shifted
In his seat you are invincible, acknowledged and unbowed.

Which to me is the description of his patent predilection
To pursue the strictest guidelines he imposed upon himself.
But what good is word selection if in striving for perfection
One obscures the human heart song
and leaves soul up on the shelf.

Banjo's subjects are not famous, nor are they entirely blameless
But their greatness he uncovers with respect and wit and grace
And they rise to the occasion on his words of adulation
That encircle our emotions like a lover's long embrace.

Ah, the man from Snowy River
on the ride that makes us quiver
And the fiery horse undaunted that he paints for us in rhyme.
Lets us glimpse them through his portal;
he has made them both immortal
As he takcs us down the mountainside
beyond the reach of time.

Where I wait, a lowly comma 'neath his monumental drama
Like Sir Edmond pondered Everest wondering will it be in vain
Yet the power of his writing keeps the muse in me relighting
And ever trying to climb into Banjo Paterson's brain.

267

THE TEN PERCENT

Ten percent of the people do 90% of the work
And they get to do it for nuthin'! And that's not the only perk,
They're asked to donate to causes,
contribute their cash and their time,
Get up early, usually stay late, and always claim they don't mind.

They serve on boards and commissions,
participate in the potluck,
Bring snacks for the kindergarteners,
for hayrides they furnish the truck
They take their turn on the fair board, as deacons or soccer moms
Jury duty or Salvation Army, ringing bells and gathering alms.

Raise funds for endless projects, the Food Bank, the FFA
Missions in far away countries, Girl Scouts and the PTA
Call on the shut-ins, fight cancer, or maybe teach others to read,
Through Rotary, Lions or Kiwanis, they work to fulfill a need.

The ten percent you can count on to sign up, to help and belong
Always ready and willing, they make our communities strong.
They often don't get the glory or noticed by everyone
But, they're easy to find at a party, doing cleanup after it's done.

What causes man to serve his fellow man? At best, I discern
Not money. Sometimes a 'thanks' is all that they'll earn.
And it can't be Evolution, where only the toughest survive,
Or lessons learned in a classroom..."Compassion, see page 25".

But it's there in certain people, giving satisfies their needs
You can't find it in a brain scan, but you can see it in their deeds
No physical exam can spot it, it won't show up on the chart
But if I had to guess what IT is, I'd say it comes from the heart.

So I'll just admit that we're lucky the ten percent are right here
'Cause without them nothing would happen,
VOL from the Greek meaning: work like a horse
UNTEER meaning; without pay

I'M RIDIN'

My Papa told a story from his childhood dust bowl days
He was out a'ridin' fences tryin' to find 'em, anyways
When he saw a cowboy buried in the sand up to his waist
Papa trotted up behind him till he saw the feller's face.
"How ya doin?" asked my Papa, careful not to be blindsidin'.
The cowboy tipped his hat, looked up and said,
"I'm fine, I'm ridin'."

As time went by my Papa grew and finally found a girl
But the big war put him on a ship and clear around the world.
Their letters few and far between were sweet in many ways
She would write him love and kisses and inquire about his days
'Bout his health, and meals and mental state
and how he was abidin',
"Don't worry, Darlin' I'll be home" he said, "I'm fine, I'm ridin'."

Back home they bought a little place and started raisin' cattle
And corn and kids and country, never saw life as a battle
But a chance, an opportunity, took the bitter with the sweet.
So busy with their daily chores just makin' loose ends meet
Sometimes they'd pass each other like two ships at sea a glidin'.
He'd peck her cheek, she'd squeeze his hand, "We're fine,"
they'd say, "we're ridin'."

Their life went by and they got old and then she had a stroke.
He held her till the medics came but ne'er a word she spoke.
He prayed like he had never prayed to heal the one he loved
And when the wheel chair brought her home
he thanked the Lord above.
"I've been so worried," he said in tears,
her smile began to widen.
He touched her face and read her lips, "I'm fine," she said,
"I'm ridin'."

Some will see their life half empty, some will see their cup half full
Some will only open one eye and find living miserable
But if yer fine and ridin', you can see and you can plan
'Cause life's got a lot to offer, if yer head's not in the sand.

All through my poetry books I have used voluminous illustrations, and for good reason, they bring my written words to life. I include those cowboy cartoonists who have sacrificed their reptuations as serious artists, to paint and draw the less romantic side of a cowboy's life.

Prominently featured in this collection are Charlie Marsh, Donny Gill, Bob Black, Dave Holl, A-10 and Bill Patterson.

In addition, many other good cartoonists have illustrated my stories in multiple publications. There have been easily hundreds of illustrations by this talented band of non-conformist cowboy types who suprise me daily with their insight and ability to draw what I'm thinking!

They are as integral to my books as the quizzical tales and questionable rhymes. My plastic sleeve is off to you sourdough sketchers, you cowboy cubists, and you wielders of the hot iron and airbrush! Thanx for always making me look good!

CHARLIE MARSH

Charlie welcomes the opportunity to illustrate Baxter's stories so he can draw cowboys, horses, cows and the wrecks that result when those critters get together.

He lives with his wife, Pat, a few cows, a border collie and assorted useless dogs and cats on a small patch about 40 miles south of Muskogee, OK, in what a few old-timers and close neighbors call Briartown.

DON GILL

Don grew up on the Bar 5 Ranch managed by his father north of Bliss, Idaho. He didn't have a TV or video games so drawing funny pictures on cabin walls became his pastime.

Today he manages the Gooding Pro Rodeo and spends his evenings playing Grandpa, head groom to a horse-crazy daughter, and #1 fan to his youngest son, who's a championship bareback rider in college rodeo.

BOB BLACK

Nurse Johnson walked slowly into the room, a squirming bundle in her arms. She looked reluctantly into the eyes of the tired, attractive woman who occupied the white bed, "I'm sorry, Mrs. Black," she said, "It's a Bob." Bob is a primate who lives in the rich arroyos of central Arizona with his wife, Stephanie.

DAVE HOLL

Dave lives on the other side of the dry end of Aravaipa Creek in southeast Arizona . . . runs a few cows . . . shoes horses . . . builds a little fence . . . does some farmin' & daywork for several outfits. He often wonders "YR he here?" but has no plans to vamoose as it is the only home his dogs have ever known.

271

ETIENNE "A-10" ETCHEVERRY

A-10's art career started as soon as he could hold a pencil . . . he's drawn on "real drawing paper," mine production reports, oilfield water ticket books, telephone directories, bar napkins and bathroom walls.

Etienne has had grand adventures rodeoing, truck driving, potash mining, raising kids and is currently a beloved art teacher in Truth or Consequences, NM.

BILL PATTERSON

Bill has owned his own art and design studio for 35 years. He illustrates annual reports, corporate image materials . . .and has illustrated two children's books for Baxter.

He currently lives in Oklahoma City, OK.